The Covert Narcissist

Recognizing the Most Dangerous Subtle Form of Narcissism and Recovering from Emotionally Abusive Relationships

Dr. Theresa J. Covert

© Copyright 2019 – Dr. Theresa J. Covert - All rights reserved.

The content contained within this book may not be reproduced, duplicated or transmitted without direct written permission from the author or the publisher.

Under no circumstances will any blame or legal responsibility be held against the publisher, or author, for any damages, reparation, or monetary loss due to the information contained within this book; either directly or indirectly.

Legal Notice:

This book is copyright protected. This book is only for personal use. You cannot amend, distribute, sell, use, quote or paraphrase any part, or the content within this book, without the consent of the author or publisher.

Disclaimer Notice:

Please note the information contained within this document is for educational and entertainment purposes only. All effort has been executed to present accurate, up to date, and reliable, complete information. No warranties of any kind are declared or implied. Readers acknowledge that the author is not engaging in the rendering of legal, financial, medical or professional advice.

Table of Contents

Introduction 4

Chapter 1: Who are covert narcissists? 10

Chapter 2: Who could be a covert narcissist? 20

Chapter 3: Who is their supply? 24

Chapter 4: How to recognize a covert narcissist 28

Chapter 5: The manipulation 49

Chapter 6: The isolation 68

Chapter 7: Stages of a relationship with a Covert Narcissist 73

Chapter 9: Attempts to leave 94

Chapter 10: What triggers narcissistic behavior? 99

Chapter 11: The aftermath 105

Chapter 12: The road to healing 111

Chapter 13: When does healing begin? 114

Chapter 14: How to deal with a narcissist 131

Conclusion 137

Author's Note 141

Introduction

If someone had told me that the man I intended to marry and spend the rest of my life with was going to turn out to be my worst nightmare, I would never have believed them. Even when it all ended, it took me a long time to admit to myself that what I experienced was not love. It was anything but love. Back then, I truly thought I was so blessed to have met him. There wasn't a shadow of doubt in my mind. I was this big idealist in love, and he was everything I ever wanted in a man. My family and friends loved him as much as I did. And who wouldn't? He was a great conversationalist, had a stable job, was humble, eager to help and unafraid to shower me with the affection I always craved for. The term "covert narcissist" wasn't even in my vocabulary, but that, of course, changed as I desperately searched for answers. I found the answers. It took me a good while, but I found them.

This "eureka moment", the realization that who I was dealing with was a covert narcissist, did not come fast, but it came, and it made me cry. I finally had evidence, an explanation that what I felt was valid. I wasn't out of my mind. And I felt the same every time I found a new answer. Then I discovered not only was there an explanation behind my pain and confusion, but that there were other people who battled the same demon, in shockingly similar ways. I talked to therapists, I read books, I met many people, of both sexes, from various backgrounds and from various age groups, who could point out identical patterns and reactions in their covert partners, parents, siblings, bosses or co-workers, as I could in my fiancé. I was unfortunate to have lost most of my important social connections during the time period of the relationship, and my whole healing journey was a push and pull between desperation to move forward, and inability to do so.

It took me a while to come to terms with the fact that losing friends and severing ties with family members was unavoidable when I didn't have the energy to maintain healthy relationships, because I gave it all away to the one that was dysfunctional. Dealing with a narcissist cost me my mental health, self-esteem, relationships, my career, and most unfortunately of all, it made me lose trust in myself.

What I find to be the most horrific thing about narcissistic personality disorder, particularly abuse imposed by a covert narcissist, is that it is invisible and thus can last for years. It is never out in the open, direct, and "in your face". It takes a lot of direct exposure to it to just get a hint of what type of person you are dealing with.

Covert narcissism is a pathological behavior that is far more damaging than any other psychological disorder, only because of the fact that it is almost impossible to recognize at first. Many survivors who shared their stories with me spent decades with a covert narcissist. That's how long it can take to uncover them. Someone who has no experience with these kinds of people and no background knowledge will most certainly fail to recognize their malignancy. Explaining why you feel and act the way you do, after being abused by someone like that, is like telling people you've seen a ghost. The person you are describing, in the eye of the outsider, does not fit your description. You just seem paranoid. As if you're a delusional person who imagines things. And that's the saddest thing about it. It is also the reason why covert narcissism is more malignant than most personality disorders. You barely make it through life, you are left with no energy to move forward, and all the time you are battling an invisible enemy no one believes you are battling against.

The invisible narcissist leaves no visible marks of abuse on their victim, but the feeling you get from it is that you feel rotten and dead inside. That is the closest that I can describe it. That's how I felt for two years constantly, and then for at least three more years I had similar random flashbacks. Inner peace and mental clarity are priceless, but that is exactly what you get robbed of when you love a "covert".

Nowadays, I can use the knowledge I gained through dealing with such a toxic, abusive and self-serving individual. Over time and through healing, this experience has helped me spot manipulation, even after just one conversation with a person, and thus helped me build healthier relationships for myself. I am no longer afraid to cut people out of my life, which was a big step for a timid person like me.

I made a promise that I will never allow myself to be mistreated, used, and devalued the way I was. With effort, I've managed to keep that promise till today. It has taught me to stop trying to put my needs in second place so as to please everyone; and most importantly, to trust myself, something I didn't know how to do from childhood onwards.

At times I wish I could just go back, "un-meet" him, and erase everything from my memory. At other times I'm actually grateful for the turmoil he put me through, because I would never be where I am in life now, if I hadn't experienced that abusive relationship I had. All my relationships after that one were only better, never worse. I can proudly say that I love my life and love myself. I am happily married, love my job and love my friends. I grew a lot as a person as a result of the trauma I've experienced. Just to remember how I used to think, "I will never find love if I let go of my covert," gives me chills. I wish I could share this energy I am feeling with everyone who is struggling to move forward, and tell them: not only is everything going to be fine, but it's going to be much more than that. It is going to be peaceful.

This book is my aim to do so, to share what I have learned from many survivors and mental health professionals who I met on my long healing journey. It is meant to help you understand that there is an explanation for the toxic atmosphere you lived in, and to help you understand it was never your fault. I hope it helps you on your healing journey and gives you some encouragement to move forward.

You will learn in depth about narcissists' manipulation techniques, their patterns, why they behave as they do, how you can heal yourself, and much more. I hope this book validates your feelings, as much as the books I read and stories I've heard validated my experience. I will be happy if it helps you make even a small step forward - because once a covert narcissist befogs your mind, every step forward will be crucial.

Chapter 1:
Who are covert narcissists?

Have you ever encountered a person who started off as being your colleague, friend or partner, who would listen to you, help you and cheer for you, only to realize - months, even years later - that they never really cared about your wellbeing the whole time? Someone who you believed was on your team, but turned out to be the person who - as time went by - made you feel guilty, drained, or as if you weren't good or attractive enough? If not, then you are the lucky one. If yes, you are a strong person who has dealt with, or suspects that he or she is dealing with, someone psychologists call a *covert narcissist*.

Covert narcissism is a type of what is called "Cluster B personality disorder", that describes a person who exhibits a series of recognizable narcissistic traits, with some of the most distinctive ones being lack of empathy for others, and quiet superiority. Although it has roots in childhood, the first definite signs start to show as the disorder develops in the late teens and early twenties, after which it continues to progress. To really understand what this means, it's important to dive into what narcissistic behavior really is at its core, first, as all subcategories of narcissism, including covert narcissism, revolve around the same personality traits.

Some might say a narcissist is a person who loves themselves a bit too much. And while this is true, when it comes to this personality disorder, things are not that simple. In popular culture, narcissism is usually associated with a group of personality traits, such as extreme self-centeredness, a grandiose sense of self, of one's achievements and looks. But, in psychiatric practice, this phenomenon goes a lot deeper than an inflated sense of self-importance. The main reason why it is so hard to spot a narcissist and then define one lies in the fact that there is not only one parameter by which a narcissist can be defined, but several distinctive parameters. So, what is narcissistic personality disorder all about? psychologists look for these traits:

- If someone in your environment seems to pay attention only to how they feel, discarding everyone else's opinions, feelings and thoughts, you might be dealing with a narcissist. A narcissist has a lack of empathy for others, and takes into consideration only their own needs and wants.

- A person who is willing to achieve their goals at all costs, even if that means manipulating others or disrespecting their boundaries so that they can get what they want, could possibly be a narcissist. Their primary focus is on themselves, and themselves only.

- Someone with a narcissistic personality disorder often indulges in daydreaming about having all the power, and being high above everyone else instead of being equal to others. This is frequently followed by the firm belief that they deserve nothing but the best, and that nothing below perfect suits them, be it social status, career, romantic partner, or group of friends.

- Because they are "above everyone else", narcissists tend to think that they are entitled to be treated as such. They see themselves as special, and deem others as average, not good enough, or "below my league". Naturally, such an individual is often described as arrogant, which is evident in the way they treat others. Everyone who doesn't like them is, in their eyes, envious and hateful, because they are not nearly as beautiful, talented, or successful as the narcissist is.

- A narcissist desires approval and wants to be admired, no matter how big their achievements are. As a matter of fact, they want to be recognized as superior even when that superiority has no firm foundation in reality. If someone in your circle expects to be recognized as the most talented, the most beautiful, or the most successful person - no matter whether that is objectively true or not - you might be dealing with a narcissist.

Not all of the above are equally present in an individual narcissist's behavior and persona, as there are different levels and types we can speak of. While in some more severe cases all of these are very noticeable, in most cases it takes some time and expertise to diagnose someone as a narcissist. When it comes to types, there are a few classifications out there, with the most narrow being the one given by James F. Masterson, which differentiates narcissists into two categories: the "exhibitionist" and "closet" subtypes. The exhibitionist subtype is the so-called "extraverted", *overt narcissist*, the one that we think of when somebody mentions the word narcissist - the person who seems to tick all the above-mentioned boxes of personality traits, as they openly display them. Frequently, with overt narcissists, what you see is what you get. With "closet" or *covert narcissist* types, this is far from the truth.

Hiding behind the mask of a sensitive, empathetic type that cares for others and their wellbeing, closet narcissists also believe they are important and special - just like overts do - but unlike their extraverted brothers and sisters, they don't show it openly. Because overts usually have open displays of their own grandiosity, it takes less time to see their narcissistic traits and therefore avoid them. With coverts, this game looks a bit different. In many cases, they appear to be quite the opposite of what a movie-version of a narcissist looks like, which is why it may take years for them to be recognized as such. All that exists in our classic, overt narcissist also exists in the second type as well. The difference is in the expression of pathological traits.

What they have in common, and what is related to their lack of empathy, is how they view other people. Not only do they believe they are higher and better than everyone else, but they see people as sources or supplies for their narcissistic needs. Because their self revolves around the belief that they are superior, powerful and worth admiring, they, as such, need an audience to cheer for them, like a star needs his or her fans to thrive in the world of celebrities. A narcissist, no matter the type, thinks as a predator: and you are their prey.

Both overt and covert narcissists are damaging to people they associate with. Both exhibit narcissistic traits, both have a lack of empathy, and both have all other traits common for this disorder. However, here is the catch - covert types are the narcissists in disguise. And that is where their power for destruction lies. As a matter of fact, these types are those that can have the most devastating effect on others' wellbeing, solely from the fact that they are not easy to spot. Most of the time, it is quite the opposite of easy.

"Socially acceptable, a person who others usually respect and believe to be one that can offer support and guidance." This is just the role they are playing. And you'd better believe it, they've rehearsed it many, many times. It is a skill they have mastered because they know the best way to get what they want from others is by making others feel safe around them. Once you meet them, you will rarely get the red flags you'd get with the other type, since they know very well how negatively people can react to open displays of arrogance or superiority.

These individuals, deep down, also believe they are special and better than everyone they have ever met... but somehow, the world overlooks their uniqueness and above-average qualities. But you won't hear them blurting about it. Not in the beginning stages of your relationship with them. They actually care what you think of them. Yet this is not because they want to inspire you and truly care for you, but because they want you to approve them. And trust me, covert narcissists will go the distance to get this approval. They need to feel validated, and the best way to do that is by making you feel like you are important, talented, listened to, cared for and understood - which is exactly what *they* want from you.

Are you still not sure how this game works? It might comfort you to know that even many psychologists get carried away by their charm in the initial stages of psychotherapy - that is, if they ever get to therapy.

By making you feel safe, important, praised and appreciated, covert narcissists buy themselves a seat in your group of friends or associates. What they give you in the first months or years of knowing them is exactly what they want from you - and what they will demand you to give them later on. Their attention and appreciation of you in the first stage is their way of ensuring what we call a "narcissistic supply". But, because of their ways of ensuring such a supply, after the *love bombing stage,* their strategy will change, and people who are their targets will experience a new and different attitude from the "covert", as we can call him or her.

The real danger of encountering them lies in the fact that they act like someone you'd love to have in your life. They are kind, dedicated, cheer for you and know how to make you feel special, so who wouldn't want them in their life? This is their mastery of charm, that will, however, be present throughout all stages of a relationship with them. In the beginning, they will use it to win you over; and by the end, they will use this charm to turn yourself against someone you should love and trust the most - yourself. This is when a covert's allure joins with another trait of theirs used to control their supply, and that is passive-aggressiveness. In turn, passive-aggressiveness becomes the covert's main tool for gaslighting, a process we are going to decode in the text that follows.

What is common for victims of narcissistic abuse, especially for those who have suffered the abuse from a covert narcissist, is low self-esteem, guilt, shame, a poor self-image, despair, depression, anxiety, self-doubt, insomnia, trust issues, isolation, and even paranoia. In the majority of cases, the narcissist was someone very close to the victim, such as a parent, a sibling, or their apparent best friend, which is why having one in your life can be so devastating. These are the people who were always supposed to have your back. Unfortunately, sometimes that's not the truth.

If everything you have read so far sounds too familiar to you, I hope it brings you relief to know that what you have experienced, or are experiencing, is not something you are imagining. You are not going crazy. You have been "gaslighted" as every victim of narcissistic abuse is. It might comfort you to know that you were chosen by them because you are a worthy supply: not because you are worthless, crazy, oversensitive, unattractive, or anything else they made you believe you are, once the bliss of the initial stage of having a relationship with them fizzled out. What you need to know is that narcissists pick their victims only if the victim has something to offer, be it your optimism, intelligence, empathy, status, money, or your good looks that they used to show you off. Or all of the above...

Many who are or have been in a relationship with such a damaging individual were living or still live in a state of denial, because covert narcissists are manipulators of the first class and will twist the mind even of the most intelligent person. So, don't beat yourself up! You are not alone in this, and we will bust the "covert" together, understand who they are, but most importantly focus on you - and how you can heal from such toxic energy that only a covert narcissist could bring into your life.

In the book, I will use the terms *victim*, *target*, and a *survivor* to describe someone who has been or is dealing with a narcissist. A victim and a target, because that is how the narcissist sees their supplies, and survivor because that is what people who have experienced narcissistic abuse truly are. Brave people, who unfortunately had to cross paths with these toxic individuals and fight to keep their light shining even in the darkest times.

Take a breather, and let's decode them so you can understand what kind of individual you were dealing with. Here we go...

Chapter 2:
Who could be a covert narcissist?

Unfortunately, a narcissist could be anyone. They play roles in various walks of life, and can be not only our lovers and spouses, but colleagues, friends, neighbors, or even family. The impact of a narcissist increases the more a person encounters them. The more we form a bond with them, the more effect they will have on our lives. In all scenarios, we don't choose to be close to a covert narcissist - we are either raised by them, seduced by them, or have to work with or for them. Every setting is different, but a narcissist will always remain dangerous, toxic and manipulative, no matter what the formality, level, or closeness in your relationship. The tighter the bond is, the greater the damage a narcissist can do, which is why it is particularly hard to grasp that someone as close as a mother, a father, a sibling or a spouse, is actually our greatest enemy.

In the family circle, for example, just like in many other settings, covert narcissists are restricted in their behavior, so it is unlikely that anyone who is not part of the family will ever notice the narcissistic patterns. These parents are usually very socially acceptable, likable, display themselves and are perceived as perfect parents and members of society. However, behind closed doors they expect perfection from their kids, wanting them to cater to their own needs and to fit into the idea of an ideal child, shaming individuality and authenticity. It is not uncommon for a narcissistic parent to project their unfulfilled ambitions, expectations, and desires of social success onto their children, putting a lot of pressure on the kids to achieve success, usually at the expense of a child's happiness.

For narcissists, kids are just tools, narcissistic suppliers who are obligated to reflect their parents' false sense of greatness. Here are some sentences these parents say to their children: *I do all of this for you, and this is how you pay me back? You are never going to be successful. No one will ever like you if you behave that way. You are worthless. I can't believe you are my child. Why can't you be more like me? You can never do anything right. Why can't you be more like your brother? You always fail me. You don't look very feminine in those clothes.* The message they send is always the same: If you don't do what I say and want you to do, you are a bad child, undeserving of love, and worthless. These parents are never focused on a child's happiness, but on their own needs and how others perceive them. Ultimately, they never have their child's best interest at heart. However, they will make it seem like their child's happiness is the most important thing in the world. They impose their will, control, and manipulate children's lives in a way that suits them. If a child fails to fulfill a covert parent's expectations, they get shamed, punished, or compared to other, "better" children.

It is not uncommon for them to have trouble letting their children grow up, especially if the child supplied them with constant admiration throughout childhood. A narcissistic parent will sabotage all their attempts to become independent and lead a life on their own. It is as if kids must make decisions under parole, hearing words like: *You are not ready for such a huge change. How could you survive on your own? You don't even know how to iron a shirt. You don't have to work, I will pay for your hobbies.* These kids grow up to be unsure of themselves, feel infantile, and incapable of making wise choices or any choices at all. In such parenthood, there is no space for following one's passion, but there is immense pressure to fulfill unreasonable expectations. As a result, children don't feel heard, and become conflict-avoidant, anxious, rebellious, or suppress their needs, all of which sadly breed more narcissistic abuse in the future. What many grow up to realize is that it was their parents - people who are supposed to be the ultimate caregivers, people everyone depends on in childhood and doesn't get to choose - who turn out to be the most toxic people in their lives.

In the workplace, the narcissist will try to dim your light, kill your motivation, discriminate against you, undervalue your work, or take credit for your ideas or achievements. The narcissistic neighbor will lie, accuse you, spread horrible rumors, disrespect your privacy and property, try to turn everyone on your street against you, or complicate your life with legal matters. A narcissist posing as a friend will put you down, ignore your needs, lie, shame your emotions, and maliciously undermine your happiness or success. The effect is always the same - you will feel undervalued, bad about yourself, feel unheard, unappreciated, ashamed, left out, or guilty simply for having your own feelings, thoughts and needs. Even for just being yourself.

Chapter 3:
Who is their supply?

Why me? Why did they choose me? I can't believe I was so naive! These are some of the thoughts that keep survivors of narcissistic abuse awake at night. If you are one, know that there were one or more good reasons a covert picked you to be their partner. And no, you were not naive.

Narcissists can't feel empathy, don't trust others, and don't believe in equality: so naturally, who would be the perfect match for them? You guessed it right - someone who knows how to love, is empathetic, kind, trusts others, and treats them as equals. A narcissist will never allow themselves to have a partner that is not worthy in the eyes of the public, as they care deeply about what others think of them, depending on praise and admiration. That being said, someone who they target is usually very intelligent, self-confident, attractive, charismatic, ambitious, or financially well-off. Or has all of these traits... Because they can't care for others themselves, they instinctively target someone who has a lot of love and is not afraid to give it.

Reliable, loyal and dedicated. These are traits everyone would love in a partner, values worth admiring, and a narcissist knows how to spot the real deal the moment they see you. Many survivors of narcissistic abuse later regret being so open and trustworthy, closing themselves off to others and to love, losing trust in people, which is very hard to regain. These are just some of the consequences of close relationships with such damaged individuals. Although a bittersweet truth, the very fact that they chose you to be their target speaks of your huge personal potential and value. Behind the mask of a charming individual is an empty shell, a vacant person who needs to feed on others to fill that void. Because they are so self-focused, they need someone who is agreeable and easy to get along with; and because they are manipulative, they need someone who is open, direct, and honest in their demeanor and communication so they always know where they're at with you.

Learning that you were just someone's narcissistic supply is very devastating, especially because it is the survivors that gave their all and invested so much of themselves in the relationship. It's very common to get into an endless loop of self-blame or even self-hate once the nightmare is finally over. Many survivors struggle with self-confidence, need some time to regain a sense of personal integrity and independence, and have a negative self-image, doubting their intelligence, abilities, strength or attractiveness. This is normal, because a relationship with a narcissist twists the reality and reverses the roles for a while. After a period of abuse, it is the survivors that feel empty, drained and hopeless, with nothing left to give. Notice the roles reversing? This is because an empty person like a narcissist needs someone who will cherish them; and this can't be anybody, but only a top-quality supply of warmth and love. As predators they feed off all the positive in others, thanks to others, and naturally, because they don't give back in return, they leave their survivors feeling empty, which is exactly who a narcissist is - a vacant person. However, unlike coverts who will never be able to love and trust, their victims can heal successfully from the abuse and get back on their feet, usually stronger than ever.

What narcissists and their targets have in common is that they are both idealists, who dream of perfect love and perfect life, but they do so from completely different stances. While coverts believe they are superior and deserve only the best treatment, their victims dream of ideal love because they believe in love and humanity.

If you feel alone in your experience, know that there are others who, just like you, had the misfortune of a narcissist crossing their path. Stories of survivors are different, but their personalities are always exceptional. Some report that they had a bad family history, were neglected and felt unloved as children, or had some childhood trauma. Some have narcissistic parents, whereas others come from families that made them feel secure, and simply had no experience of these kinds of malicious individuals. Whatever your background, know that it could happen to anyone - being chosen by a narcissist is not a sign of your weakness or naive personality. On the contrary, they would never pick someone they know will break easily, because they feed on strength. Men and women with a well-rounded personality and praiseworthy traits naturally attract other people, and unfortunately, narcissists are some of them.

Chapter 4:

How to recognize a covert narcissist

Understanding and uncovering a covert narcissist is never easy. Partially from the fact that the way you felt in the beginning stages of a relationship does not match how you feel in the final stages, and partially because not all of them exhibit narcissistic behavior to the same degree. However, all of them harbor certain traits that are specific to this personality disorder, and most of the time these are recognizable only once the "devaluation stage" kicks in.

Unfortunately, the narcissists around us can be people we are deeply involved with, which is why our judgment is clouded by emotions and loyalty to them. Frequently, survivors of narcissistic abuse were raised by covert narcissists, only to end up in a relationship or marriage with another covert, or find themselves befriending narcissists. No matter who the narcissist is in one's life, they always have the forementioned narcissistic traits in common. The only thing that is different in each case is the setting or area of life where the narcissistic abuse takes place. The best way to uncover one is by examining how they make you feel. Here is what coverts have in common:

Projection

Behind the mask of a confident, charming person they display to the world, a covert is a deeply unsatisfied, and in their minds, misunderstood personality. While some coverts are somewhat consciously aware of this feeling of inadequacy, guilt, and shame, in most cases this plays out in their subconscious minds. Because they reject or deny these feelings, the only way they can make themselves feel better about who they are is by making you take on these issues. It is a very common occurrence among narcissistic abuse survivors to harbor self-hate during and after the relationship with such a damaging individual. Once the healing process takes place and the covert is out of their lives, survivors' minds start transforming into clarity - it was never them, it was the individual they were dealing with. By projecting insecurities, identity issues, fears, shame, guilt or anger onto you, coverts make themselves feel better - more superior, in control, and better than you.

How it works: Let's say you are a naturally lively person who likes to socialize and go on adventures. You love investing time and money into new experiences, and enjoy having a good laugh. As you are getting to know them, a covert will tell you how much fun you are, and accompany you to parties. However, once they get you hooked, they will stop laughing at your jokes, will refuse to go on adventures, and will cancel plans at the last minute. A covert will do so with a blank expression on their face, or rolling eyes, as if your suggestions were boring. Every healthy person will feel inadequate and shameful. Are you indeed boring? Maybe you have lost the spark? This is exactly how they want to make you feel. What lies behind that change is how they feel about themselves. A covert narcissist is not as much fun as you are, but they would like to be, therefore the only way to make them feel better about themselves is by reversing roles. If you feel like you are the boring one, that means they are more fun than you. Here is how they use projection for their benefit.

What a covert says: *You always imagine problems, it's like you don't want our relationship to work out.*
The reality: You are noticing how something isn't right in the relationship and are trying your best to communicate your doubts to your partner, in order to make the relationship work and resolve issues. They are the ones who don't want to work on the relationship: but are paranoid about the idea of you leaving them. As a result, you will feel guilty and paranoid for bringing up issues.

What a covert says: *I'm afraid you are going to leave me. Are you lying to me?*
The reality: They want to make sure you are a secure narcissistic supply while they are probably the ones lying to you. By justifying themselves, they are reversing roles and transferring all suspicions from them, onto you.

What a covert says: *You only care about how you feel.*
The reality: They don't care about how you feel at all, and will make you think that you are selfish for considering your own requirements and wants, which need to be discussed. To enjoy a healthy relationship, this has to happen in order for those needs to be met. In this way, the focus goes back to them.

The "Chameleon Personality"

They know how to talk the talk, seeming to be great conversationalists and quite charming when you first meet them. However, their charm comes with a special catch. Coverts are people who have no clear identity. Therefore, every interaction they make with others, be it professional or personal, is a different version of themselves; an adaptation to current circumstances and people they presently interact with. They are very skilled at observing what it is that other people value, what their likes and dislikes are, and according to the information they gather by observing, they simply blend in. It shouldn't surprise you to find out that they were never into indie movies, sports, or music, as you thought they were in the initial stages of the relationship. Taking on other people's interests and their persona allows coverts to take the relationship to the next level, to create a bond with others, and secure narcissistic supply.

Someone who is unfortunate enough to spend years with a covert narcissist can start noticing how this process works. Whenever they are among new people or simply different settings, they act differently, and have no consistency in interests. In fact, their interests seem to shift rapidly, which is not to be confused with a healthy curiosity. They don't have a strong sense of self, or the personal integrity a mentally healthy person has. Many of them are smart people who will do proper research on their future "victims", especially if they sense someone will be a really good, solid narcissistic supply. Remember: a narcissist doesn't care about your needs, wants, and interests - unless they can find a way to use them to their own benefit.

Infantile impulses

Somewhere along the lines in this text, there was a word or two, a hint about the way they react when they don't get what they want. The infamous silent rage and passive-aggressiveness they harbor is a covert's way of projecting their negative emotions onto you. Because the outer world doesn't acknowledge how superior and special they are (as they see things), they constantly feel undervalued and angry at everyone who doesn't give them the time of day. You, probably the only person, or one of the few carefully selected people who have the misfortune of seeing this part of them, will get the worst end of the stick. By giving you the "silent treatment" every time you do something wrong, or even when someone else does them wrong, they will get you hovering between trying to figure out how to cheer them up, trying to please them, and figuring out what is wrong. This game can go on for days and leave the other side feeling very distressed. Robbed of the ability to empathize, and unable to rationalize their actions, narcissists react with high emotional immaturity in what are triggering situations for them. Let me give you an example: Chris recalls how distressing one of his attempts to leave a covert girlfriend was.

She would cry hysterically, almost like a child who wants their toy back. There was a mixture of fear and anger in her eyes that I have never seen before, it reminded me of the Twin Peaks episode where Bob finally gets uncovered in the jail cell. It was a scary thing to watch. She walked around in circles, then grabbed my arm with a tight grip; I could almost feel her nails piercing my skin. I couldn't believe I was looking at the same girl who had showed zero interest in the relationship for the whole time, standing in front of me and weeping like an infant, throwing things around. I felt sorry for her and stayed in the relationship, only to learn months later that that was a terrible mistake. Twice she repeated a similar performance, after which I finally terminated the relationship for good.

Although not a general rule, some narcissists do become physically violent, while the majority usually use insults to hurt the other. Because of their inability to cope with stressful situations, which is due to their lack of maturity or ability to relate to others and effectively learn from painful experiences, they firmly hang on to passive-aggressive behaviors.

Taking instead of sharing

Relationships are a two-way street, but in a relationship with a covert narcissist, that is never the case. Yes, "it takes two to tango", it's just in this case one person needs to fully adapt to the other, regardless of how they feel and what they think about the dance the two of them are performing. The relationship with them is based on imbalance: they take and never share, or if they do share, be assured they are doing it just so they can use it against you later. They take your time, energy, money or body as they please, and you'd better not complain about it. Sex lacks intimacy, doesn't make you feel loved or bonded, and your bank account is theirs as well. If you don't give them what they want, many will sulk like little children, have rage tantrums or give you "the silent treatment". In their mind, you are just a property, an object they hold onto tightly, something which helps them satisfy their needs. Ultimately this makes their victims feel extremely devalued, affecting their mental health drastically. Because they know how much drama saying "no" to the narcissist brings, they give in to what the covert desires and wants, in the hope that doing so will keep the peace and save the relationship.

The most unfortunate thing is that they do this behind closed doors, when it's you and them only, so even if you try to confide in someone about what you are going through, the chances are not many will believe you. After all, he or she is the kind and charming one who cares about your wellbeing, right?

The polarity

When Jenna confronted her husband and the father of her children for not responding to her calls when he goes on business trips, he told her that he thinks it is healthy for the relationship not to stay in contact all the time. He claimed it should be the time they each take for themselves, and that she should lead a more active life and get a hobby, instead of checking up on him all the time when he is traveling. However, once she actually started practicing yoga and going out with friends when he was away, he started blaming her for acting irresponsibly by not calling him to check if he arrived safely and to say how the kids were doing, claiming she must have found another man.

Don't be surprised if you get blamed for doing what they advised you to do. It might have suited them once they said it, but later, once it doesn't, they may make you feel guilty for doing it. Polarity is not only about not keeping promises or sticking to what they said. Coverts are good with words, and know how to get under your skin, saying just the right words to get things to work in their favor. They frequently don't follow through, whatever it is they said or promised, and they will twist the truth so it suits them. By giving logical, seemingly full of understanding explanations of why they are behaving the way they are, or apologizing, they intend to calm you - and get away with unacceptable behavior. Of course, this makes you try to rationalize things, especially if the topic was something that bothered you about them, or the state of the relationship, and ultimately brush it under the carpet. They readily make promises or make you feel heard, only to do quite the opposite - because it suits them. As a result, you feel confused, not knowing what to trust. or how to approach the same problem. With them, many times things don't add up, and they use this approach just to hush your comments on the situation they are in, if they feel exposed or attacked. Ultimately, their actions and words are contradicting, because many times they say appropriate or loving things just to take you off their to-do list. They say they will make the effort, but they never do.

The self-absorbed personality
Their self-centered personality becomes obvious months after the survivor of narcissistic abuse starts healing from the damaging relationship with a narcissist. Unlike overts, who usually openly show how self-obsessed they are, this group

will show glimpses of their ego-centrism through disguised actions. Those who had a narcissist in their life describe how confused they were when the person who seemed to care about their wellbeing, the self-sacrificing person who they trusted, turned out to be nothing else but self-absorbed, egocentric. And this is something the victim could only realize once the narcissist got a one-way ticket for leaving their life for good.

Loving ourselves first so we can love others is a good thing, a healthy thing to do. However, the mind of a covert functions a bit differently. The only person a narcissist cares about is themselves and themselves alone - and this is where their capacity to love ends. The only needs that must be met are theirs, and their perception of things is always better than yours. Combined with well-developed manipulation tactics and the ability to project their own issues and fears onto their victims, they achieve their ultimate goal, which is to bring the focus back on the only person that matters - themselves.

They don't care how you feel, but will make you feel guilty for feeling anything at all unless the feeling revolves around your admiration of them. And you'd better believe it: they have no real, genuine desire to know you. However, being master manipulators, which is something we will talk about later, they know how to put on a show, and they are able to do so in whatever way it takes to make things look as they see fit or necessary. Many of the survivors hold onto their memories of good times with their abusers, blaming themselves for the failure of a relationship.

Maybe I should have been more caring. If only I had put more energy and effort into the relationship. Maybe I was selfish for asking for more intimacy in the relationship. Maybe I asked for too much. These are just some of the questions victims of narcissistic abuse keep ruminating over after a breakup. But the truth is, only a healthy person who knows how to genuinely care and empathize with others can ask themselves these questions. A covert will make you feel like you are never enough, and yet you will even have sleepless nights thinking about what you could have done better to make it work. You could have done nothing. If you are asking yourself these questions, know that you probably already gave too much. Even if you died for them, they wouldn't find it to be enough!

Your orbiting around me 24/7 is not good enough: try harder. This is their mentality.

They have no desire to know you. They don't care about your day at work. They don't care about your problems, and they will show you this by engaging very little in things that matter to you - or not at all, making you feel weak or guilty for even bringing up things that matter to you. In a healthy relationship, you would never feel this way.

Manipulation and lying

Covert narcissists are masters at playing with your mind, to the point that you question your own actions, thoughts, memory, and even sanity. They know "mind games" very well and are not afraid to use them. This is extremely devastating for one's mental health, and even seemingly small things can be used as a base for getting their needs met by tricking or lying to the other. They need to be the ones who have total control over the relationship and ultimately, over their supplies.

These are the *"means justify the ends"* kind of games, and because there are so many ways they can manipulate you, this book has a whole chapter dedicated to this subject. A narcissist has no boundaries, and will take what he or she wants from you, be it your time, money, your space, belongings, empathy, and even sanity. They are master manipulators who know exactly how to turn the people who are their supplies against themselves - while looking innocent all the time. They take advantage of and use people for their own gain. They know how to turn every situation in their own benefit, and even go as far as making their target look crazy and paranoid in the eyes of the public, while displaying themselves as victims. Their actions leave you with a lack of clarity and install doubt in you, because your having clarity is a potential threat to their stability. This is because their stability is based on you giving them what they want. For them, other people are just tools that help them achieve their goal; and using others for their own gain is a consistent pattern of their behavior.

Conditioning

Because connection with a covert narcissist is muddled by their behavioral patterns, with them, the relationship feels like a contract where nothing is given freely, be it love, affection or time. In this sense, everything a covert does for you is always done strategically, so they can benefit from it later and gain control over the relationship. As a result, the whole relationship feels restricting. Coverts use fake compassion, altruism, and empathy to get under your skin. One of the strategies coverts rely on is offering help and guidance at any time of the day, especially when you don't ask for it; be it help with things that make you feel extremely stressed, or simple daily tasks. They will pay for your drinks, help you with work, or even take on whole tasks for you. Some will offer to yield you money, pay your bills, or talk to your boss on your behalf. These kinds of behavior are exactly what distinguish coverts from overt narcissists - unlike overts, they act as the very opposite of self-absorbed.

By doing things for you, they accomplish two things. One, they get you to trust them and make you believe they genuinely care for your wellbeing; and two, they install guilt in you and weaken your sense of healthy independence, which is a weakness they can use to manipulate you. They did so many things for you, so naturally, you feel the need to repay them somehow for all the care and kindness they have shown to you. As a result, the relationship loses the natural flow of giving and taking. To have a balanced relationship, a healthy person will respond to these altruistic behaviors with the same level of altruism, but because the covert has apparently done so much, the other person feels pressured to balance the scales.

This creates a "loop of guilt" and forms a relationship that is based on conditioning, and not on unconditional love as it seemed to be in the beginning. By doing this, a covert ensures you will do anything they ask from you, once you catch their delicious, altruistic bait. Although they do use words when conditioning their victims, many times they won't even have to say the words like *I can't believe you are so selfish: I did so much for you and this is what I get back. You don't care about me at all; I can never rely on you. I was always there for you any time you needed help. I gave you all my love and time, and you can't help me with one little thing.* Their victims will naturally feel pressured to give the covert whatever it is that they need.

The wise critique

Unlike the overt narcissist who would openly put you down and discard your efforts, with coverts, things get a bit more complicated and a lot more undercover. Their aim is to lower your self-confidence by taking the role of a wise teacher who only wishes the best for you. They are the one who knows everything, and you are an infant who is unable to deal with the world around you. When they are around, you simply won't feel supported or protected, and you won't be able to pinpoint exactly why. When someone else criticizes you, they will not come to your defense. Under the mask that they want to help you learn important life-lessons and give constructive criticism, is a strategy to make you feel undervalued, incompetent or immature, while they appear wise and mature, no matter the actual age difference.

No matter how good you are at something, and no matter how hard you are trying, in their eyes, you can always do better. They will criticize you with special gusto if they notice you're trying really hard and exhausting yourself, under the pretense that they want to push you forward. This is a frequent trait of covert parents, who will act disappointed and withhold affection from their kids if they fail to satisfy the impossible criterion of perfection. Once you do succeed or get an amazing idea, they will make sure to let you know what their contribution to your success was, or even steal your idea. Taking credit for what someone else did is also not unexplored territory for them.

Drama

Narcissists drain your energy. Because they operate as parasites, your peace of mind is their food, and they need to make something dramatic happen to feel important and alive. Some will flirt with others in front of you, spend the money you saved together, spread false stories about you, or turn your loved ones against you by describing you as difficult, drama-oriented, or mad. Life with them is not peaceful: many narcissistic abuse survivors recall that such relationships are like walking on eggshells, as there were tiny details that would disturb the covert. There was no healthy communication, and many describe arguments with them as drama for the sake of drama. Some would come to your friends for advice about how to "deal with you", telling them you are cheating, inconsiderate, or selfish; and they will do so with the same innocent face they had when they met you. Combined with their passive-aggressiveness, they would sometimes even make you lash out at them, wanting an explanation for the silent treatment they gave you, only so they can accuse you of being the one that rages and likes to fight. The distance they are willing to go to feed off your energy and disturb your life is frightening.

Sabotage

The irony, or rather a painful truth, is that victims of narcissistic abuse ruminate a lot about what they did wrong in the relationship, when they were the ones who were "full in" and trying to make the relationship work. They sabotage everything you care for, your relationship with them included.

Once the initial stages of a relationship end, and their devaluation of you starts taking its toll, it is never the covert who tries to talk about problems, gives thoughtful gifts, focuses on possible solutions, compromises, plans for a date, fun time, or anything else that is important to keep the relationship going. As a matter of fact, they are not interested in healthy relations at all - which is why they won't try to fix it, work on it, or make it better. Once their victims catch the bait, a narcissist will leave it all up to them and won't move a finger. Because a close relationship is supposed to make you feel happy, naturally, they won't put in the effort.

They don't want a stable, healthy, drama-free relationship. A covert narcissist is not interested in your happiness, as they see any positive emotions you go through, anything that makes you feel stable and joyful, as a potential threat that will empower you and take you, their narcissistic supply, away from them. Therefore, they will sabotage everything you care about, such as a need to heal or be nourished as an individual, be it in your career, a hobby, friends, or sex, which they will withhold from you. They do this by using projection and some of the manipulation techniques I will go into later. Some coverts will go as far as turning the "little people" who support you in everyday life against you. Others will look for flaws in what you do, and lavish you with pessimism.

Covert narcissists are jealous of everybody's success, and you are not an exception. Although they will never display that openly, they will do little things to undermine your happiness, either by withholding support, by giving you backhanded compliments, or destructive criticism.

Either way, they will make sure you are never better than they are... because the only person that deserves to be praised is themselves. They won't celebrate your success; they won't be there to cheer for you on important days. Your success awakens the deepest insecurities in them, and because they see the world as an opponent they compare themselves to, they won't enjoy being under the rays of your bright, shining light.

Detachment

Amanda recalls: *Looking back, there was something about him that made me feel alienated and understood at the same time. His words were comforting, but there was something missing in his expression. Now that I think of it, I never felt he genuinely cared about what I had to say. That's what was missing, the genuine connection.*

Cold, detached, uninterested, and emotionally distant. These are just some words used by people who had a covert in their lives. A relationship with them is clouded with a lack of freedom to express oneself. The spontaneity of a relationship and its natural flow are rarely present.

This is because a covert needs to feel in control, and to stay in control they need to detach. They create emotional distance, yet use their charm to talk the right talk. The relationship lacks intimacy, be it mental or physical or both. Even when they confide and open up, the conversation feels more like a philosophical discussion than a genuine connection.

Chapter 5:
The manipulation

The mind games covert narcissists play consist of many tactics they use to shift your view of reality to their own benefit. Control over the relationship and over the other person they have an intimate relationship with is of crucial importance for their survival. This is why they have well-developed, underhanded, concealed manipulation techniques that are difficult to recognize. These behavioral patterns include playing with someone's mind, conspiring against the other, devaluing, blaming the other and many more, all of which are used to confuse, distract, and attain control. The danger of these games is that they have serious consequences for the person they are practiced on, in some cases even leading to suicide. A covert narcissist is a very malicious and toxic individual, and here I am going to list some of the common manipulation games they play on their victims.

You must be going out of your mind: that never happened

Jennifer always kept her clothes tidy and in one place. She never had trouble with losing or misplacing her stuff, until she moved in with her sister. She began noticing her clothes were missing and asked her sister about it, but she would always give Jennifer a negative answer. *I don't know. You must have lost it/misplaced it.* After a while, she started noticing her sister's perfume or the smell of cigarettes on her clothes. At this point, once asked about it, Jennifer's sister would say things like: *Don't blame me for your lack of organization. Who knows where you were? Try remembering things a bit better, and stop blaming others for your lack of memory.* Sometimes she would be angered or irritated with such questions, raising her voice. She would even go as far as saying things like: *You are imagining things again. Oh, don't you remember? You lent me that jacket for my night out on Friday.* Jennifer couldn't recall such agreements. After a while, she began questioning her own judgment and sanity. *Maybe I did forget. Maybe she is right. What is wrong with me?*

In reality, nothing was wrong with her. She was not crazy. Jennifer never actually borrowed her sister's clothes, and her sister did take her things whenever she needed them. What she was experiencing is known in psychology as *gaslighting*. It is a process when one manipulates another person who is their target by denying, shifting blame, or negating the truth. As a result, it causes their victims to question their sanity or memory. This is very damaging to one's mental health, as the victim starts doubting their own reality, what they saw or heard.

In the workplace, gaslighting can manifest in many different ways, from a covert narcissist taking credit for your achievements and ideas while convincing you that you had nothing to do with it, to concealing important information and turning this against you. They won't tell you about the changes in schedule, cancellation of projects, new rules or strategies, only to have you breaking the rules or putting effort into a project that is canceled or paused. Once you make a mistake, they will kindly tell you about the rules or changes, with words like: *I told you about it,* or H*ow can you not remember? We discussed it twice already* - and similar convincing acts. The goal is always the same, and that is to sabotage you, make you question your own memory, competence, abilities, and sanity. In the process, they will look like a professional, caring, "hero archetype", and you will look like a mess in front of your colleagues.

They will be the dedicated ones, the ideal team player, who wishes only the best for you and the company, no matter if they are your teammate or a boss. Meanwhile, you will be stressed, exhausted, start losing self-confidence, and think you're going mad. The most unfortunate thing is that very few people, if anyone at this stage, will believe you even if you start suspecting something is "off" about the covert narcissist, and not you. After all, they will do anything to make others like them, and will use this charm even on your loved ones if they have a chance, only so that everyone plays on their side, which only enhances the effects of gaslighting.

Contradicting words and actions
Remember that we talked about how unstable a narcissist's persona is, because they become who they are with? Their lack of identity allows them not only to adapt to the target and present the desirable traits, but it also helps them attain control. How? By being as equally fluid with actions and words. They don't have a sense of morality, and therefore their values and opinions change based on their current needs and circumstances. As a result, their partners often get totally confused when the very thing the covert said they loved about them, is what they suddenly hate. They change depending on how strong and independent you are, or are not, as well as depending on the stage of a relationship you are in.

If they say they will take you to a theater and you agree on it weeks before the show, a few hours before the show they will lay on the couch, pretending that there was no promise made. If they say they won't call you names, they certainly won't stop doing it. Maybe they will even add some new ones to the list. If they said they love your body, they will make fun of your belly when you are intimate. If they said they love your cooking, they will criticize and reject the meals you make.

The point of this tactic is to achieve two goals, hence the duality. The first one is to "buy" you with the first action, and the second is to make you feel confused, distort your perception, and play with your memory. The first action, affirmative action, is there to make the other person give in and trust that the narcissist loves them, because people naturally care the most about the opinions of those they are close to. The second, of course, is taken to gain control. A narcissist's words don't match their actions, but their victims usually never realize their behavioral pattern because a covert is good with words and knows exactly what to say at the right time. They don't care about staying true to their promises, but only about being exposed, being confronted, or losing narcissistic supply. At the very last stage of a relationship, when a victim's first few, usually unsuccessful attempts to break up with the narcissist occur, it is frequent for a narcissist to play this game. They promise they will be a better, more caring partner, that they will improve intimacy or be more open, stop mistreating, cheating or lying. Once the dust settles in and narcissistic supply is ensured, all the words become erased.

The game of "hot and cold"

Here is a short story: Nicole and her boyfriend didn't go on a date for some time. One night, Mark, her boyfriend, took her out to her favorite expensive restaurant, and they laughed, flirted and kissed all night long. She felt invigorated and loved. The feeling lasted for two days. On the third day he was cold and distant, just as he was for two weeks before the date. This pattern went on and on in their relationship for months.

This relationship is based on giving crumbs of affection and attention out of a covert's free will. Since the narcissist has ensured they have gained the other person's trust by lavishing them with constant affection, admiration, and love, they can securely switch to playing this game. It is based on a past memory a victim has of good times with a narcissist, and careful dosing of affection. By doing the bare minimum they keep their targets hooked. The target is left confused, yearning for love and affection, which gives the manipulator full control over the relationship because it is they who have the power to give or withhold love and affection. The other person feels unloved, unworthy of love, or thinks that there must be something wrong with them because the narcissist has stopped loving them. With this method, a covert devalues his or her victim, sending a message to the other person that they are not lovable.

Many times, victims feel drawn to try harder to make the relationship work; believing their partner, the narcissist, is losing interest. Once they feel all hope is lost, and contemplate giving up trying, or leaving the relationship, the narcissist kicks in with displays of love and affection, only to lure the other person back. When the victim is lured back in, they can safely return to being emotionally detached, until the next "red alert" their supply gives them. In psychology this is called "intermittent reinforcement", and it is a process where the free flow of love and affection is restricted, and replaced by careful dosing of love in order to attain control over the other and the relationship.

The game of targeting weakness
We all have something we don't like about ourselves. In a healthy relationship, our partner, parent or friend will accept

us for who we are and cherish our imperfections. In a relationship with a narcissist, that is never the case. Targeting their victim's weaknesses and insecurities is used to trigger self-doubt and lower self-esteem. They can trigger you either by actions or words, but the results are still the same. It's all in order to make you feel infantile, like you are not good enough or lovable enough. Sometimes they will be very upfront, for example telling you to lose weight or stop embracing yourself. What may seem like a constructive criticism coming from the person you love, is actually a malicious attempt to make you more conscious of your dissatisfaction with your body, or your social anxiety. They don't do that because they want to help you become a better person, but because they need to feel better themselves. While these comments are usually very direct, they have still mastered the skill of putting you down without being too obvious. Sometimes, however, they target weakness more subtly, such as in these examples:-

You know a lot about engineering for a person with your background.
That makeup is amazing; you are completely transformed!
That outfit really makes you look skinnier, you should wear it more often.

I am sorry for interrupting you at work: I thought your job isn't so consuming.
You look like a real man next to that car.
Congratulations on your speech; you appeared very self-confident today.

These comments are meant to put down, degrade, and are disrespectful and insulting to the person they are directed at. What makes them so demeaning is the fact that they are wrapped in the sheets of honesty. Compared to upfront insults that are easier to be recognized as hateful, these so-called left-handed compliments make the target really think the "truth" behind "compliments" reflects how others see them. A person who is made to believe there is something wrong with them, particularly if that is reaffirmed by someone they have trust in, like a narcissistic parent or a long-term partner, is easier to manipulate.

Apologize to me because I hurt you

Max wanted to start a family business, and open a hostel in the unused part of the house where he was living with his mother. To use the space, he needed her legal approval as the owner of the house. She never gave him the permission he needed, but kept nagging about how incompetent he is. When he got a position in France, she blamed him for leaving his ill mother alone and thinking only about himself. When he confronted her about her behavior, this is what he got: If you really wanted a career as much as you claim, you would get it regardless of what anyone else thinks, and you would find a way to do so.

Because nothing is the relationship is ever their fault, naturally, they need to twist the reality in order to make it work for their own benefit. They do so by shifting the blame to you, even if they are the ones who cause your heartache. A covert does something hurtful or inconsiderate, and they get called out about their unacceptable behavior. To defend themselves, they will take the focus off themselves by blaming you. The process includes both negating the truth while refusing to take responsibility for their actions; and deflecting, which is changing the course of blame and transferring it to the other person. Here are a few sentences people who dealt with coverts had to hear:

I wanted to talk to you about it, but you are so oversensitive, I didn't want to hurt you.
I flirted with that girl because you made me feel unwanted.
I didn't put you down. Why do you always want to make me look like a bad guy, when I care for you the most?

Any intelligent person who reflects on their own actions will start questioning whether the narcissist truly gets the point. The initial confusion after such deflecting leaves the narcissist enough space to shift the focus onto the other person. Be it putting their targets in the defensive mode *(I am not oversensitive)*, making them question their behavior and actions *(How did I make you feel unwanted? Why did you feel that way?)* or simply making the target look like a bad guy who needs to apologize *(I am sorry; I know you care for me. I guess I was just triggered)*, their targets feel a mixture of confusion, anger, conflict, guilt, shame, and a variety of other negative emotions.

Everything is your fault

Like previous ones, but far more upfront and nonetheless equally hurtful, is the "*everything is your fault*" game. One thing they love doing is shifting the blame to the other person, and because people they have close relationships with are usually empaths when blamed, they will feel guilty. Anyone who has a narcissistic parent or spouse knows how it is to feel guilty for something they didn't do or couldn't change: *I couldn't live my life because you were born. It is your fault I'm not successful. It's your fault I slapped you yesterday. It's your fault we don't sleep together any more.* The list goes on. This way they turn their partners or children into scapegoats. It is an escape mechanism they are not aware of, by which they express dissatisfaction with themselves by blaming you for their own bad behavior. You *triggered* them. You *caused* it. It's not they who are mistreating you, it is you who cause that behavior, otherwise, they would never act that way. The interesting thing is that this "blame-game" can be practiced only on self-aware people who are naturally focused on bettering themselves and their relationship, because someone who is not self-reflective won't bite into it, which is exactly why narcissists pick intelligent and empathic victims. Frequently, they use blame as a counterattack, or simply to lash out at someone because deep down they believe the world is unjust to them, and doesn't acknowledge their brilliance.

Covert narcissists have a "victim-mentality" combined with an extreme superiority complex, and since their targets are always caring, loving people, it is easy to slip into narcissists' guilt-tripping game. Their targets genuinely want to make the relationship work and make their partner, parent or boss happy. Unfortunately, with a narcissist, whatever may be said or done, it is never enough. Nothing can satisfy their egos, and there is no amount of admiration, love or appreciation that will make them respect their targets. Because of this mentality they crave approval, and if they don't get it, they will make you feel sorry you didn't obey their irrational, grandiose demands. In a family where one parent is a covert narcissist and there are children, it is not uncommon for one child to become the "golden child" and other the "scapegoat". The scapegoat is the child who gets blamed for wrongdoings and mistakes made by others, and it is usually the child that, unlike the golden child who successfully fulfills a narcissist's desires, doesn't want to obey their demands or become the perfect child the narcissist expects them to be. As a result, they get shamed for being authentic, for not being as good as their sibling, and get frequent, unjust punishment and abuse as a result.

Covert narcissists are skilled at distorting reality and will know exactly how to use your actions or inactions against you. Again, like other manipulation techniques, this is a way of making you feel small, and because you are small and powerless (read: guilty) that means they are better than you. Even more, you are presented as an obstacle to happiness, and not acknowledged for all the efforts you put in.

I know what you need to be happy, so I am not going to give it to you
Probably the most undercover manipulation technique psychologists allude to, when discussing the narcissistic

personality disorder, is withholding. To be able to withhold something, they first need to be in the role of a provider. While one provides, the other is in a constant state of lack and depends on their provider's willingness to give them what they need. Because a healthy relationship is not a trading deal, they need to make up the goods they will bargain or withhold from the other. Although some narcissists provide financially, others use different resources such as praise, affection, intimacy or support, which is cruel and extremely depriving. In loving relationships, these things should be equally provided to both parties without conditioning, but with a narcissist that is never the case.

A narcissist won't cheer for you, support you, or do anything else a loving partner should do. They will do the opposite, and even punish you solely for the sake of ruining your happiness. Since their expression of dissatisfaction includes a spectrum of passive-aggressive behaviors fueled by silent rage, they will punish you for being successful, self-assured or enthusiastic, simply by not joining you in your happiness. Did you get promoted? They won't give you a pat on the shoulder but will be moody instead, or whine about their bad day, only to kill the joy. Did you make an amazing acquaintance? They will make sure to go the extra mile to detach from you that day. Withholding revolves around silent punishment for something you have never done, and they make their partners feel like love is too much to ask for. Passive-aggressiveness causes the other person to feel like a burden to a narcissist, as if what they are hoping for is too much. This is possible thanks to the so-called silent treatment, which is a tool that helps in shifting the focus back onto the narcissist.

They are very aware of what their counterpart needs to feel fulfilled in a relationship, but because the happiness of the other, in their eyes, takes the control away from them, they resort to holding back and denying the other whatever it is they crave the most. All the survivors of narcissistic abuse remember living with a constant yearning for closeness and intimacy. One of the big issues therapists highlight that all narcissists have in common, is their inability to feel close to people and experience intimacy. This is why some ex-partners describe sex with them as "robotic and soulless". They felt like intimacy was just a task a narcissist wanted to tick off as quickly as possible, without giving them any warmth, or caring about pleasing them.

Sex is a natural component of a relationship, something that helps us bond with the other on the deepest level, but with such an individual, and just like all other areas of relationship with them, it lacks in closeness, and feels unpleasant or restrictive at the least. It naturally provides pleasure and contentment, which is why they withhold it. Many narcissists use withholding intimacy as a way of making their counterparts feel unwanted and unattractive, which drastically changes their self-image for worse. It's painful because it feels like you are not deserving of pleasure. They take you and your body in the sense that you are there to please them, and they never please you. Just like the emotion of love and honest devotion you have for them, narcissists use intimacy to manipulate you and take away your personal power and enjoyment. Many women I talked to who dealt with a covert told me they could never relax during sex with them. They felt constricted: it's as if their body knew something was off, way before their rational mind did. When you feel safe and loved for who you are, you have no trouble enjoying yourself in the arms of your partner. A narcissist will, just like with everything else, make you feel it's your fault you two are not intimate frequently, and will do so without saying so. And just like with any other area of your relationship, sex too will revolve around them. They will take you when they want you, but perhaps will reject you when you crave them. After all, all they need to do is not make you feel loved in their arms, while you are in their arms.

It's always the "little things" that make you feel unwanted. The lack of foreplay. No eye-contact during sex. No kissing. No cuddling. As the effects of love-bombing start to fade, sex with your perfect partner, who is so compatible with you, will feel different. They know you depend on them for sexual pleasure, and because of their complete, cruel detachment during intimate moments, and your feeling like something is wrong with you and your body, you probably never get pleasure in the relationship, and dare nor seek it outside. And if you have sexual fantasy and you tell them about it, rest assured that the moment they "fulfill" it will be the moment it won't be your fantasy any more, because of how uninterested or bothered about it they appear. They will never say it, but you will feel it is off.

It is not uncommon for survivors of narcissistic abuse to be embarrassed about their physique, even though there is absolutely nothing wrong with them. As a matter of fact, many men and women who were in a relationship with someone having narcissistic personality disorder are attractive people, as a narcissist will never allow themselves to be with someone who doesn't boost their status that way. First sexual encounters with the next partner, who is not a narcissist, feel so relieving and empowering, it almost makes you cry for joy. The very fact that the sexual dysfunction you believed you had for so long, and your inability to orgasm, is wiped away once you begin healing is one of the happiest, most freeing acknowledgments you'll ever have. That's how depriving a relationship with someone who has a twisted, narcissistic mind can be.

Some other techniques recognized in people with this personality disorder include reduction mechanisms, overly dramatic displays, and using other people to manipulate you. The *reduction technique* is based on invalidating and downplaying the emotions, perceptions, and thoughts the other person is experiencing, followed by blaming them for being overly dramatic or oversensitive. This results in the other person closing in and isolating themselves, feeling unheard and misunderstood. Because the narcissist doesn't intend to deal with anyone else's feelings and needs but their own, they will find the quickest way to stay in control of a situation, which is by invalidating the importance and intensity of their partner's feelings. Contrary to this, when it's their emotions in play, they blow things out of proportion and show glimpses of narcissistic rage, which we will discuss in the next chapter. Since their partner is viewed as their property, it is important to minimize the influence of other people on their target. Although not all narcissists do this, those who do have a hazardous effect on the interpersonal relationships of anyone related to their target, as well as the target himself or herself. They act as a medium between a few or more people, creating a "hate triangle", where the narcissist plays the game of being a shoulder to cry on for both sides, and then uses the information or creates false information to make a feud between two people. In this way they not only create a false image of their target but also create a solid ground to isolate them, all in order to be the biggest influence in this person's life.

All techniques are based on their desperate need to have power in any given moment, because showing love and kindness is perceived as weakness and makes them feel subordinate. They feed on and indulge in fantasies of ultimate power, domination, seductiveness or authority, and therefore they see other people as their opponents, rather than partners. The relationship is hence a power game, not a medium for interpersonal growth.

Chapter 6:
The isolation

It felt like I had no life outside the relationship. I had very few friends at the time. That relationship was my whole life. I felt as if no one understood me. I felt like I didn't matter. This is how life with a narcissist feels like. All survivors I had a chance to talk to say that a relationship with a narcissist made them suffer loneliness and isolation. While not a direct manipulation technique, their isolating you from friends and loved ones is a form of control. The process of isolation is complex and includes a few elements, which are: your glorified perception of a narcissist, triangulation, and all the forementioned manipulation techniques combined.

Being involved with a narcissist means the whole focus of the relationship is on them - and this leaves little to no space for other people in your life. Gaslighting and the drama you are pulled into demand a lot of personal energy, and leave none for other areas of life. On top of that, the partner you are investing so much of yourself in is giving nothing in return, feeding you crumbs of affection when they find it suitable. A person with NPD (narcissistic personality disorder) will first make you believe you have found your soulmate, and because they are so helpful and loving, no other person will be able to compete with the amount of affection you are receiving from them.

In the romantic relationship or also in a work setting, in the beginning, there is a natural inclination to spend time with the newfound ideal partner or do some extra work for the best boss you've ever had. However, the first red flags show as early as this infatuation stage.

The narcissist asks to spend more and more time with the victim, or does more not-asked-for favors which innocently put them in the spotlight. They become someone you love to spend time with, and often choose not to say "no" to. As time goes by, these favors and showers of love will slowly become debts to repay, and which leads to you circling around them, trying to make them happy and invest in the relationship.

You are pulled to invest more and more, until you come to the point where you start losing touch with other people and your own identity slips out of sight. Once you're at the point where their manipulation develops and advances, you are already too invested and too emotionally and mentally worn-out to deal with other people.

Someone with NPD will make you feel constricted to express yourself, and will do so with passive-aggressive tantrums and the "blame game". Survivors explain that talking about their issues felt like they were being a burden on the narcissist, so they would just rather keep everything in. The blame game, underhanded comments, and emotional detachment will make you want to be stoic and strong, so as to not be perceived as overly sensitive or over-dramatic, which is what they want you to think you are.

Isolation, however, becomes larger-scale and affects a victim's relationships with others. Due to psychological triangulation, a process where the narcissist includes a third party in their relationship with the victim, the victim loses connections or reputation in society.

The narcissist aims to weaken their supply's support network, as this gives them more power to influence their target's life and manipulate them once other people are out of the equation. They do so by acting concerned for your behavior, health or wellbeing. This is what they'd say to someone:-

I'm concerned about her mental health and I don't think she will listen to me, so please, if you can talk to her about it. I feel so hurt because she blames me for flirting, but she is my whole world. I would never look at other women. I am afraid he is hiding something from me: he is acting distant towards me. He yelled at me yesterday; I am so scared to talk to him now. I am just concerned about those friends she hangs out with: they seem to be a bad influence. He is just so negative lately; I can barely talk to him. She won't be able to come to your party: she is too tired from work thesedays and needs some rest. She is only focused on her work; she barely has time for our children.

While these sentences may seem like expressions of real calls for help, genuine care, and pure emotion to an outsider, they are always twisted truths or pure lies that serve the covert to create a bad image of you, so you lose your support system.

Unfortunately, this may work even on your closest associates such as friends and family, as these people, just like you, know how to love and trust. Because they love you, they will believe the narcissist must have a proper reason to be concerned, and they will come to you with the image of you the narcissist has projected onto them. A narcissist will usually back their lies with real, rare events the person who they are trying to triangulate with could witness themselves. Events are, of course, taken out of context to serve the narcissist in creating an "anti-you" scenario. This makes the story even more convincing.

As a result, their victims face rejection, feel isolated, misunderstood, confused and excluded. Many don't have a clue that the narcissist has included the third person to create these twisted truths, just because the narcissist seems so genuine. This is how they create their enablers, their *flying monkeys*, as we name them, recalling the assistants of the Wicked Witch in "The Wizard of Oz".

These are people who enable narcissists to proceed with their malicious acts, and continue with devaluing and abuse. While not having malicious intentions themselves, flying monkeys choose the side of a narcissist, many times not knowing they are doing so.

Instead, they truly believe they are being helpful. In the process, the narcissist will seem completely innocent, like they had nothing to do with how other people see you. You may be very surprised by how people start acting towards you, and this can drain you and make you feel even more alone.

Chapter 7:
Stages of a relationship with a Covert Narcissist

A relationship with a narcissist doesn't have a natural flow, and is characterized by stages that are absent in healthy relationships. The natural balance of giving and taking is disrupted, and relationships with such individuals start with infatuation and idealization, only to end in devaluation, rejection, and complete discarding of the narcissist's partner. In psychological and therapeutic practice there are three main stages of a relationship with a narcissist identified, and these are the *idealization phase*, *devaluation*, and *discarding*.

Idealization

During the idealization stage, the narcissist earns their target's trust by showering them with affection, appreciation, praise, and adoration. They lift the other person up, cheer for them, offer unlimited support, a shoulder to cry on, act as a friend in need, and a perfect lover who just knows how to make things right. This is called love bombing. During this phase, it is a narcissist's aim to recreate the ideal relationship, and earn the trust and loyalty of their targets.

Covert narcissists have a fluid identity that allows them to transform like a chameleon and adapt to any person they are with, in order to gain their respect and trust. They are perceptive, analytical, and will investigate the target carefully, in order to create the perfect scenario that ultimately gives them the green light to move on to the next phase of a relationship, which we will soon describe. It is in a narcissist's interest to be liked, and so they create a "persona" that is likable, since the only thing they care for is admiration. This first stage is about them taking on their target's identity in order to get the admiration they believe they deserve. The behavior almost resembles a teenager who desperately wants to fit in with a group of popular people, just to be popular and liked themselves. Coverts' emotional detachment and infantility allow them to reflect the person they are with, quickly attaching their needs and wants to the other person - they are giving because they know it will be appreciated, and make them likable. Needing acceptance and admiration from you, a narcissist will do anything to get it - and will go about it so smoothly you will hardly notice they are mirroring who you are. In other words, they will do it covertly.

The love bombing is based on acts and words of adoration that are excessive and "too good to be true". The survivors of narcissistic abuse often say that their relationship with a covert was like heaven in the beginning:-

It was perfect. It felt like a fairy tale. Our relationship was ideal. I thought I'd finally found someone who gets me. They made me feel special. They seemed like the person I have been waiting for all my life. I thought I had finally found my soulmate. We were the best couple. We had so much in common. Back then I felt so lucky I'd found them.

They know how to target your weaknesses and use them to manipulate you, at this stage by earning your trust through building you up in those areas you feel insecure about. When love bombing, they will idealize you and the relationship, make you feel very special and worthy of love, only to make you feel completely opposite at the next two stages of the relationship.

It is a very common thing for survivors of narcissistic abuse to say that they were very impressed by the way their covert had the same interests, lifestyle, and hobbies as they did. A narcissist does detailed research on their targets and will spend time learning about and absorbing the interests, tastes, likes, and dislikes of their victim. While there is a natural inclination people have to be open to learning about the interests of people they like, in the light of a narcissistic personality disorder this is not a result of curiosity, but a lack of identity; and the desire to be desperately liked and worshipped. Many love-bomb others by taking care of their needs, giving them gifts, compliments, praise, taking them to places, or being overly helpful even when there is no actual help needed. This behavior has a certain level of pushiness, but because it seems genuine, the person who is being love-bombed perceives the narcissist as the nice person who just wants to love and care for them. Many of their former partners say they actually felt inexplicably uncomfortable for receiving so much attention, and somehow needing to return the affection or favors, but couldn't recognize it as a "red flag" back then.

Ultimately, in the love-bombing stage of a relationship, the narcissist treats the other person as if they were the narcissist themselves. Although it is never a conscious process in their mind, the person they are targeting is seen as an extension of themselves. In the beginning, this person is the extension of their praise-needy, self-important, "ideal" side of the personality, a boost to their ego that shows how valuable they are. The other person is a "replica" of themselves, and they are a replica of that person: their interests, thoughts, and feelings. This process is called "mirroring" or projecting the aspects of self to the other person. However, it is a two-way street, and so at this first stage, the target of a narcissist will feel very special, beautiful, respected for their talents, important, or praiseworthy - which is exactly what a narcissist thinks about themselves.

Everything they do they needs to be returned, and in double or triple doses. If they do a lot of helpful things for you in the beginning stages of a relationship, rest assured they will require you to do little or big favors for them - and make you feel guilty when you are not able to put a pause on your life and deliver what they need, when they need it. The idealization phase is a base a narcissist builds for themselves to create a safe zone where they can be admired, while gradually revealing their true selves as the relationship progresses. The paradox of this disorder is because the narcissist knows that the way to connect with other people is to be open, empathetic, and interested in the other person; and yet they use it to create an environment where they can be who they are - the un-empathetic, closed-off person who doesn't care about the other. The final goal is to make the target comfortable enough so they can gradually refocus the relationship towards themselves.

This stage, just like the other two, is as present in work and family environments as much as it in love relationships and friendships. For instance, covert narcissists are often praised and respected members of society, many of whom are very involved with charity work, or hold important positions. They care about their status, and what others think of them, so naturally, many will opt for careers that allow them to be in the spotlight in one way or another. Covert colleagues and bosses will be the first ones to hop in to help you with tasks, help you get things done, and even take your part of the job on themselves. This, however, lasts only during the first stage, when you get to know them. They appear agreeable, kind, generous, charismatic, and everyone seems to love them. Remember, no matter what place they take in your life, there are always three stages of a relationship present. Don't be surprised that once the appreciation-bombing phase is over, you suddenly get criticized, unappreciated for things you were once praised for, or if they take the credit for your ideas or give it to someone else. They want your full trust, and will give you praise and help whenever you need or don't need it, only to twist the reality and diminish your ambition, work drive, and health, later on.

Devaluation

It is at this stage where little things they adored about you suddenly become flaws and something you should be ashamed of. Once the relationship is established and the covert has created a safe haven by gaining your loyalty and trust, they gradually start expressing their dissatisfaction with the relationship and with you. Because they have first carefully analyzed your weaknesses and built you up, they will start using your fears and insecurities against you. Although never or rarely openly, they slowly diminish their target's self-confidence by planting the seeds of self-doubt, fear, and even self-hate in them. This happens periodically; it is hard to pinpoint and even harder to understand, because it is done so subtly and still entwined with sporadic acts of love and kindness, especially at the beginning of this stage.

The trouble here is that a covert narcissist devalues their partners subtly and appears completely innocent in the process. More often than not, this devaluation manifests in little things they don't do for you, rather than the things they say directly and openly, especially at the beginning of this stage. Because it is a covert narcissist we are talking about, this phase can revolve simply around them not acknowledging your needs, wants and desires, showing less and less interest in your life, and in you as a person. They will not shout, be cruel in obvious ways, yell, or say mean things. Instead, they will damage your self-esteem in little, subtle ways, later turning to more serious manipulation techniques mentioned in the previous chapter. Devaluation can go from little things like not replying to text messages, not calling when agreed upon, or prioritizing other people or things; up to giving silent treatments, criticizing, nitpicking, or blaming the other. The reason for devaluation is to make them feel better about themselves, because that is the level of emotional immaturity the narcissist operates on.

In the workplace this can manifest as falling from being the number one worker, to the average one; or maybe comparing you to, or praising other employees who put in less effort than you do.

At the beginning of his career at the company, Richard was his boss's favorite employee, always prized for his ambition, problem-solving skills, and efficiency. It was his dream job, so he tried his best to put all his enthusiasm in it. However, as time went on, he could hear his boss complaining about the little mistakes he made in the projects, the tidiness of his office, or his time-management. These were nothing new, but unlike before when such tiny mistakes weren't regarded as major, which they were not, they were now seen as Richard's lack of professionalism and capability to meet required criteria. He did extra hours and took on more responsibilities than he should have, to prove his dedication, only for his boss to blame it on him for not finishing, even more.

A narcissist will not invite you to their birthday party to which everyone else is invited, under the excuse that they want to celebrate with you in private. They won't go for drinks with you, but they will do so with everyone else. They will claim they miss you, but never call you to come over, or make the effort to come and see you. They'll invite you as their special person on an exciting event, only to act like you are not even present. These and similar behaviors don't cherish you as a person or honor your place in the narcissist's life. A covert narcissist will devalue you by not respecting your time, and refusing to communicate, understand and accommodate your needs. By not making the other person feel like a priority when it is necessary to do so, they lower their value, sending the other person a hidden message - you are not important enough. As red flags pile up, now the narcissist uses strategic and sporadic acts of affection from the first stage to mask the game of "hot and cold", gaslighting, periodically giving underhanded comments and putting the blame on the other.

This process happens slowly over time, and as a relationship progresses the love-bombing acts become more and more rare, and get replaced with ignoring, aloofness, detachment, gaslighting, blame games and other manipulative and toxic behaviors. The first reactions of most victims are to go with the flow and simply repress their feeling of inadequacy that starts building up. However, because the other person is left loathing in self-doubt, as time goes by, they start over-analyzing, believing there must be a very good reason for such cold behavior. Confused, victims of the narcissist tend to spend months or even years in denial, which only prolongs this phase and causes their mental health to slowly deteriorate. They are made to believe it must be their fault that the narcissist is not prioritizing them, so they turn to self-blame, believing the narcissist is such a nice, genuine, caring person, so the problem must not be with them. Because love bombing was consistent, it is hard for the targeted person to figure out what is going on in the relationship, early on.

Maybe I am not showing them how much they mean to me. Did I do something wrong? Am I being too needy? Am I oversensitive? Maybe I am just overreacting. Maybe I am not as beautiful as I was. Maybe I should spice the relationship up a little bit.

As these and similar thoughts begin to pile up as a result of the detachment that happens during this phase, the other person slowly starts being absorbed into how they can fix the relationship with such a perfect partner, their ideal soulmate. At this point, the victim of a narcissist starts doubting their own self- worth, abilities, and talents. The covert, on the other hand, seldom appreciates positive changes and acts of love in their partner's behavior, making them feel even more unappreciated and unvalued. The more the narcissist pulls away and severs the love bombing, the more their victim becomes desperate to save the relationship, and loses themselves in the process. As a result, their victim slowly takes on full responsibility for the relationship, the household, kids, or work, with narcissists putting in less and less effort. Therefore, thinks the covert, all the bad things that happen in the relationship are to be blamed on you. Emotional manipulation allows the covert to get more narcissistic supply without even looking like the bad guy, which is the saddest truth about these incredibly toxic relationships. It is very painful for the victims of a narcissist to accept and understand how they went from being treated as perfect, to being treated like they don't matter. They may try to fix mistakes that they didn't make, try to make the narcissist happy, make them fall back in love with them or appreciate them as they once did. However, the more effort they put in, the more space the covert has to devalue - since they will feed on this effort and demand more of it, while putting their targets down as a result.

The effects of devaluation can, sadly, linger long after the relationship with a narcissist is over. Because the trust built in the first stage seems to be established on a very solid foundation, and you are made to believe that they are indeed the best person for you, who loves you so much, it takes a long time to realize what is going on in the relationship. After all, they are sometimes an attentive, caring individual, and they will give you a dose of this love from time to time, only to ensure their narcissistic supply. If and when they act attentive and loving, there are only two reasons for such behavior at this stage. One, because you have given them a serious hit of narcissistic supply, their favorite drug; and two, because they want to get something from you. Period. People who love you, if you are happy to have them at this point in a relationship, will notice something is off, your natural radiance is fading, and you are not happy. You feel bad, you are moody, anxious and depressed, but you can't explain why. Narcissists are dangerous people - and at this stage, it all starts to take a toll on their victims.

Discarding

The final, and the most emotionally and mentally draining phase, the discard phase, is when the narcissist tries to take the last bits of your energy, fails to do so, and as a result, throws you away as if you were an object that is no longer of use. This phase manifests as a sudden, and very hurtful, heartbreaking and disrespectful breakup, or a series of bad breakups. Thanks to the objectification, which allows them to see you as a disposable item rather than a human being that feels and thinks, they reject you as they please, as if the whole relationship was nothing. While it's a mentally wrecking process for their victim, for the narcissist the breakup is easy, and causes them no pain at all.

One of the reasons they can walk away with no remorse, besides their objectification and lack of empathy, is that while preparing themselves for leaving you, they have probably found one or more spare "narcissistic supplies"! That is why it is not a surprise that it is extremely common for the narcissist to hop into the new relationship just a few weeks after a breakup or divorce. In the case when you are a family member or a friend, they will find another victim in their surroundings, acting like you never existed in their lives, no matter the family or friendship bonds, which is a shock that can be extremely painful and hard to heal from.

A narcissist is a very perceptive individual, and notices when their victims start rebelling against their manipulative techniques. As a result, they resort to the next level of manipulation and take things to the extreme, perhaps threatening to leave the relationship, or in extreme cases, to commit suicide, take the children, harm the victim, or destroy their belongings. Meanwhile, because they are alert to the fact that their narcissistic supply is running out, they go out and put in an effort to find a new, better narcissistic supply. The discard phase happens for two main reasons. The first reason is the slow but steady awakening of the victim and their setting firm boundaries, and the second reason is that the victim has nothing left to give to the narcissist or the relationship. It could be that the victim isn't as good looking as they used to be, their bank account is dry, or they simply feel dead inside due to all the havoc the narcissist has caused over time. In other words, they are completely drained, can no longer orbit around the narcissist, and have no energy left to provide them with a solid narcissistic supply. A narcissist is like a parasite, a virus that damages the immune system of their host, which shows both in their victims' mental and physical health. Because they have drained their victims to the last drop of energy and robbed them of positivity and radiance, victims feel like empty shells and can even get physically sick. Narcissists are users and abusers, so they rob you of your goods, and it shows in all areas of your life, from physical appearance to lowered social status. Both reasons are equally common, and can be combined.

Once their victim starts realizing their behavioral patterns and begins to gain some insight about the relationship as it really is, the narcissist will discard them for a much easier, far less aware "supply". Because the old supply sees through them, has figured out their tricks, and their tactics don't work on them any more, the narcissist needs a backup plan, as the supply leaving them is something they will never allow to happen. The new supply requires no effort, has no firm personal boundaries, and doesn't make it difficult for the covert to get what they want, which is an unlimited amount of admiration and appreciation. When their old victim starts asking them to take responsibility for their actions or fights back, they get alerted, which causes the "fight or flight" response in them. Their response to being called out on manipulative behavior is usually an amplified blame game, when they try to make themselves look like a victim, or else a narcissistic rage.

Chapter 8:
Hoovering

Unfortunately, devaluation is not a one-time process. Frequently, it happens on and off in the form of multiple breakups followed by attempts to make it work. The trick with them is that after the breakup happens, it is never truly over, even if it was on their terms. The relationship with such an individual needs to be on their terms, from the beginning till the end, which is why they have to be the ones to leave. They can't and never will take responsibility for their actions. A narcissist will reattempt to get supply for you many times in the future, even if they are in a new relationship. This is called *hoovering*, the last hope for the narcissist to get what they want from their ex-victims. Hoovering is a narcissist's attempt to desperately lure you back in, with new attempts of love bombing, explanations, a shower of love, and new promises of hope as they tell you they have changed, and that it will better this time. It is a manipulation technique that is the last straw of hope - both for the victim and the narcissist - but for completely different reasons.

Because the victim is left completely devastated and ruined after the breakup, not knowing what has happened or how to cope with it, all too often he or she stays in the state of denial for months, even years. Denial is a powerful tool that allows them to soothe the pain, but sadly gives the narcissist a chance to get more narcissistic supply. After the breakup, many victims loathe in self-blame, think about what they have done and what they could have done differently. At this point, it is not hard to stick to the old pattern a narcissist has created in them, which is to feel responsible for all the things that went wrong. After all, it takes a long time and some bad experience with hoovering attempts for the victim to realize they have been pulled into just another toxic game. The bait for the narcissist here is the desperation they sense in their ex-victims. As long the victim has love for them and wants them back, they can come and go as they please, causing even more damage to a person who is already hurting.

The narcissist doesn't know how to love, and they will never come back because they miss the other person, but because they need them. They need a supply because it makes them feel safe, and they will not back down under any circumstances until the victim decides to cut all the possible contact with them and sets unbreakable boundaries. This is, unfortunately, a very hard thing to do, especially in the beginning, as the victim is completely robbed of self-worth, feels very rejected, unattractive, and worthless, feeling deep down like they don't deserve any better. The effects of love bombing last even till the last stages of a relationship with them, as the victims see the narcissist as a perfect, irreplaceable partner, a "one true love" for a long time - until the healing starts taking place step by step.

Comparing the victim with a disposable object in the dumpster is probably the best analogy for the hoovering or vacuuming process, as shared by one of the survivors of narcissistic abuse. A narcissist will get back to the dumpster to retrieve their former victim only once they have nothing left to eat, meaning they have run low on narcissistic supply from the new victim. If you suspect you are dealing with a narcissist in your life, as they attempt to get back in touch, saying how much they love you or can't live without you, rest assured they are never doing so because they truly realize what they've done. They do so because they are running short on the supply and need their dose quickly. Every attempt to get back together with them will be temporary, and last only until their victim starts seeing through the hoovering pattern. They never change: they just reinvent their old role from the love-bombing phase, but the smile never, ever stays on their face for too long. Here is what a hoovering scenario can look like:

What a covert says: *We can break up if that is what you decided, but I am afraid someone is going to hurt you because you are so sensitive.*
The reality: You are unhappy and would like to break free because you feel unloved and uncared for. They are the ones who will break down once you, their narcissistic supply, leaves them. They are the ones who are hurting you.

However, once the hoovering stops, be prepared to go through the roughest storm you've experienced, which is the breakup or the divorce. Breakups initiated by them feel like the last sword stabbed in your back, where you already had nine of them and were barely alive. They leave suddenly and many move on to other supplies just as suddenly, which makes the whole process even more painful. Part of the discard, no matter if you are in the process of divorce or have separated, is that you're barely breathing and almost unable to get up in the morning, and yet they're enjoying the best time of their life - this is what they want you and everyone else to believe. They are with someone else, "...finally finding happiness after a horrible marriage with you." You are the horrible, inconsiderate, selfish, crazy "ex" they just needed to save themselves from, and the sad thing is, many will believe their lies, even you. You might think that maybe you are not attractive, maybe you were inconsiderate, insensitive, needy, or anything else they made you believe.

Breaking up with you is the ultimate *you are worthless* message. Most often than not, the final breakup happens out of the blue and is such that you are left without an explanation. Once you do reach out to them to get an explanation, all you will get are insults, blaming, shaming and extreme criticism. Victims find it hard to find closure a long time after a breakup or divorce happens. A narcissist will "ghost" their spouse and not give them any clarity, which is extremely mentally wrecking. It may feel as if you are so worthless you don't even deserve an explanation. At this point, you really do feel as if you are undeserving of love.

And while their new target is enchanted by the love bombing, you are going through completely the opposite of that - and the narcissist is getting supply from both of you at the same time. Your pain supplies them, as much as the adoration the new target showers them with, especially if you get them notified about how lost you feel without them. You compare yourself with the new victim, blame yourself, or simply, as many other survivors I talked to, feel numb. The breakup they impose on you leaves you in a complete state of shock and confusion that is hard to get out of. The hoovering can start again the moment you become so vulnerable and lost without them, regardless of whether they are still with the new supply, or not. Once you show them how horrible you feel without them, they will come back and give you glimpses of hope, feeding off your energy once again. Showing them any sign of love for them, missing them or wanting to talk to them, is an invitation for a narcissist to come and get some more supply. Sadly, with them, it's always the never-ending story: and once it does end, their toxicity remains in your energy for a long time.

Chapter 9:
Attempts to leave

Hoovering can happen even if you are the one that said "no" to them. For a narcissist, this can completely throw them off balance, and they will not give up on their supply easily, especially if they haven't found a replacement and the breakup left them off-guard. If you are going to initiate the breakup, be prepared for extreme reaction, raging, begging, hysteria. or being verbally assaulted.

As their victims are perceived as objects, the narcissist feels they own them as a property that belongs to them, and therefore no one can steal that from them. It is shocking to see how infantile, yet demonic their reactions can be, especially if you tell them it's over, in their face. It is then when their true shades show better than ever.

The mix of anger and despair on narcissist's face in these situations really shows their inner world, which is dark, clouded with abandonment issues, emotional instability, and immaturity. Because of the infantility shown in these moments, many victims feel sorry for the narcissist and get pulled back, misinterpreting this behavior as a form of apology and regret.

The narcissist may indeed act and say things that a person who is regretful of their actions would, but behind their tears and begging always lies emptiness, and a weak person who is panicking, terrified to lose their source of supply.

Once the breakup becomes a real deal, when you finally see through the hoovering and you get very determined to leave them behind for good, things really start to boil. I have to tell you: Breaking ties with someone who has NPD, and doing so on your own terms, means all the narcissistic traits will be magnified and all the manipulation techniques will get nastier.

Stalking, threats, insults, begging, blackmailing, conditioning and unexpected visits, are all combined with attempts to use their charisma to turn the whole world and everyone who loves you against you.

They won't fret to manipulate your own kids and friends against you by portraying you as heartless, insane and selfish. Losing control is out of the question, and they will use all the resources they have to try to "puppet" you, be it financial stability and the home they provided for you, people you care about, or your social status.

A narcissist wants you to feel weak, and will go to great lengths to win at the breakup game, one way or another. A couple of survivors have admitted that their narcissist has even threatened to kill themselves if they leave, which is just a glimpse of what they are capable of, but they will never do it. Such a serious statement is just a way to scare you and bring you back, just a cruel game they play.

Ironically, in the best-case scenario, if you are lucky enough, they will just move on to another solid supply and leave you to heal from pain. Their replacing you with another victim and living a "perfect" life, just like you two lived at the beginning of a relationship, is just their way to punish you for leaving them.

Divorce with them is a horrible territory to pass through, especially if you were the one who filed for it. The charisma they seduced you with, and the role of caring, altruistic, honorable member of society whom everyone loves will be exactly what the judges and everyone in the courtroom and outside of it will see. In more extreme cases, for survivors who needed to battle for custody over children, the process of divorce was a nightmare, especially if the narcissist was a mother and kids were young.

A twisted mind with NPD will go above and beyond to win custody, but not because they care for children and their wellbeing, but because they want to win and make you desperate. It takes a lot of strength and support to win against them at the courtroom, be it the custody, a divorce, or property ownership, and the whole process can cost you mental health, money, and much, much more. It takes the involvement of a psychiatric specialist, a good attorney, patience, and support from friends and family to win against them.

Because they live in a constant state of fear and have such fragile egos, covert narcissists will do everything to protect their false sense of grandiosity, and don't care about how big the cost is that people around them have to pay. Your leaving them means they are not good enough, and portrays them as horrible partners to the outer world, which is something they will never allow: hence all the lies, stories about you, and the deceit. So, what is the best way to make you look bad, other than projecting all their fear, issues and rage onto you?

They will do anything to sabotage your happiness even long after the relationship ends, because your happiness is your victory, so it's not surprising to hear all kinds of horrific, untrue stories about you years after the end of a relationship.

Breaking up with them and walking away takes a lot of courage and personal strength, and although a bittersweet truth, survivors of narcissistic abuse, once they build themselves up, become one of the toughest people there are - if you survived a relationship with such a toxic individual, you can survive anything.

It's trauma, and damage of self felt on a deep soul-level, but once you start to heal, it can be a road to extreme personal empowerment, as impossible as it sounds. But it's true. The very fact that you gathered strength to say "no" to them speaks of how tough you are, so don't ever put yourself down for putting up with them. You didn't know. No one does until they experience it under their own skin.

Chapter 10:
What triggers narcissistic behavior?

All three mentioned phases are part of the narcissist's behavioral patterns and coping mechanisms. Something many survivors are curious about, especially once they realized they indeed had a narcissist in their life, is what causes the switch from love-bombing to hating and discarding? Individuals with narcissistic personality disorder have certain triggers and motives that drive them to behave the way they do. Their self-talk is not based on reality, but on delusions of grandiosity, ultimate power and superiority. In other words, they don't see themselves as flawed, but misunderstood and unappreciated for their "specialness". However, because they are human just like everyone else, they do have flaws, unhealed wounds and a lot of toxic patterns, but unlike healthy individuals who look within and try to heal, a narcissist looks outside themselves for relief. Because they believe they are perfect, that means everything that goes wrong in their life must be to blame on others. The whole relationship, during all three stages, is based on two main motives. The first one is to find someone who will make them feel special and go beyond and above to prove that to them; and the second, to find an escape from personal unhealed trauma, fear, pain or anxiety.

Unlike individuals without NPD, narcissists don't want to heal and don't see that the problem is in them. They're not willing to face their fears, which is why all their relationships will always include love-bombing, devaluing and discarding. Every "next" becomes the crazy "ex", and every new partner is perfect until they become the new crazy "ex". It is very rare for a narcissist to ever seek professional help, and if they do it is always because of something other than NPD, such as anxiety or depression. They get into relationships so they can feel worshipped, not to exchange love, which is why they usually love-bomb people who have a big heart, a lot of empathy, and know how to love.

A narcissist has a pattern of falling for emotionally open and available people, expecting them to fulfill unrealistic fantasies of perfect love and expectations of how they should be treated. Their subconscious works like this:

I am important and special, so if you love me, you will prove it to me by obeying me. If not, I will be triggered and have to put you in your rightful place. If you put your needs first, I will make sure you regret it, and treat you with passive-aggressiveness. If I made you happy, that means I put you in the first place, which means I am weak and a loser. If I am in pain, you are responsible for soothing it and you have to take it away. I need you to move mountains to prove to me how significant I am to you, no matter how you feel. And I will never give it back to you the same way, because only I am special.

Narcissistic personality disorder has its roots in childhood, and so do its triggers. All kids are naturally egocentric, but as they grow older they develop empathy for others. For narcissists, that is not the case. The roots of narcissistic behavior lie in fears of being taken advantage of, losing control and being overpowered. The uncontrollable fear of being perceived as weak, of being manipulated and used, is therefore transferred onto other people. Therefore, showing empathy, care, love, kindness and emotion, means that the other person is more important and in the spotlight, which is something they will never allow. These are their ultimate triggers, which is why relationships with them are always a power game, where they need to be the powerful one at all costs. Caring for others in their minds means being powerless, so no relationship with others can ever be based on love, fairness or equality, which are essential for a healthy relationship. They are always aiming to feel superior, perceiving the relationship as "you versus me", instead of "you and me". Everything that a healthy relationship should consist of, is what triggers them.

Since they are vulnerability-avoidant and have deeply rooted fears of being used, they are triggered by the smallest things you do and say. Anything that calls for compassion, intimacy or empathy, is deeply triggering: be it talking through problems, or making you feel good in bed. A narcissist hasn't outgrown the initial ego-centrism as other children did, which is why they have powerful "ego defenses", as psychologists name them. Just like a child who demands constant attention and needs to be praised to feel good about themselves, a narcissist reacts from ego and lives in a constant state of neediness. The outer world is perceived as an enemy, including and especially people who are close to them, so they live in constant anxiety, ready to defend egos at all costs.

Narcissists are sad, fearful people, driven by anxiety and pain. Among adult covert narcissists are many that were neglected as children, whereas some were privileged, some raised in emotionally cold families that perceived emotions as weakness, or by controlling and overly ambitious parents who demanded perfection from them at all costs. To protect themselves, children who grow up to be narcissists develop a false and grandiose sense of self, false self-confidence, arrogance, and extreme self-centeredness. They live in a constant state of fear, like a exposed nerve, ready to lash out in pain and punish those who fail to worship them.

Probably the most defeating thing about trying to invest in the relationship with someone who has an NPD is the fact that there is very little you can do to change them. Narcissists do not have the consciousness needed to recognize, accept and change their behavior - they truly believe it is all your fault and have no capability to reflect on their actions with self-censoring. Due to a lack of acceptance of their own flaws and refusal to take responsibility for their behavior, unfortunately, many of them never seek help or wish to improve. Instead, it is their victims who end up seeking help from professionals. A narcissist has a victim mentality and therefore everything that makes them feel weak and vulnerable is perceived as a threat to their ego. Just as it is with all other personality types and disorders, no two narcissists are the same, so there is a wide spectrum of narcissistic behaviors, all of which combine with different levels of consciousness. Some covert narcissists are more naive, truly living the role of misunderstood, undervalued people; while others are more malicious, more conscious, and much more damaging to people around them.

What triggers them is an injury to their false self-image and ego, and this can be anything: saying how you feel, expressing your thoughts, demanding equality, expecting affections, failing to cater to their needs, asking them to take responsibility for their actions; asking for more intimacy, setting healthy boundaries, breaking up with them, expressing ideas that don't match with theirs, not putting them on the first place at all times; being independent, failing to put aside your problems in order to focus on them and make them feel loved... The list goes on. These are all reasons for them to evaluate or discard you, whereas in a healthy relationship this would never be an issue. Because their self-confidence is based on a false image of self, the older they get, the more manipulative they become in order to protect their fantasies of superiority. Their behavior is always agenda-based and immensely remorseful: no human will ever be able to fulfill their fantasies of ultimate grandiosity, no matter how giving and caring they are.

Chapter 11:
The aftermath

The aftermath of dealing with a narcissist can be truly felt only once you go "no contact" and no longer have them in your life. The effects of narcissistic abuse are long-lasting and go way beyond any direct contact with the narcissist. Even once they are no longer present in your life, the toxic cloud above your head still remains. Gaslighting, drama, lying, isolation, and a series of other manipulation techniques we talked about leave you mentally numb to the point that even dealing with everyday tasks feels like a burden. The consequences of having such individuals in your life are many, as you are affected on all levels of your conscious and unconscious being. In other words, you feel broken and damaged in the mental, physical, emotional and spiritual planes. In addition, in cases of many survivors, the narcissist also affected their material surroundings, which resulted in a loss of friends, status, money or property.

Survivors of narcissistic abuse suffer a wide range of mental health issues as a result of long-term manipulation and devaluing, all of which have roots at the beginning stages of a relationship with a narcissist. Anxiety and paranoia are some of the most common reactions to being mentally and emotionally abused: they are all part of a PTSD (post-traumatic stress disorder). Because of the constant distress and chaos survivors have been part of, they experience flashbacks, intense headaches, have trouble sleeping or vivid nightmares. Life with a narcissist leaves our brains in a state of shock and extreme confusion, and traumatizes the mind, causing troubles with concentration and feelings of agitation. Survivors have trouble communicating, and may experience social anxiety and agoraphobia (the fear of open space and crowded places). The feeling of isolation stemming from the days of a relationship persists, and people who dealt with a narcissist feel too vulnerable to expose themselves to the outer world, which is often followed by a state of paranoia and beliefs that people are evil and want to cause us harm. It's like living in a constant state of "fight or flight".

Since gaslighting is one of the most dangerous, if not the most dangerous form of playing with someone's mind, many victims experience mild to severe disconnection, where they feel as if they and the outer world are somehow separated. Because of the state of shock, the mind activates these two coping mechanisms, which are a normal response to prolonged stress but can be troublesome if not treated. If you feel like you are an actor in your own life, a ghost of your former self, who is not able to feel or be present in reality, it is likely that your mind is just trying to protect you until you heal by dealing calmly with the reality. It is possible to feel this way even during the relationship, starting as early as the devaluation phase, in which case the depersonalization and disconnection just deepen once your abuser is gone, until you start to heal.

Another very common side-effect of being involved with a narcissist is *depression*. Survivors feel "blue", are not motivated to take care of themselves and life gets to the point where even taking a shower seems like a huge task. Depression can be mild, but unfortunately, can also be fatal, causing thoughts of ending one's life, or even suicide. Their life has been drained, and the survivor is left in a fog, with no self-esteem, no drive, and no hope for a better future. All energy was given to the narcissist and the relationship, so that they just can't find the strength to continue with their life, especially if feelings of love for the narcissist are still there. You are made to believe there is nothing about you to love. Your dreams and ambitions have been extinguished, and you believe you are not lovable unless you are perfect, or can fulfill someone's demands. You don't feel good enough, let alone capable of moving on, so who wouldn't feel depressed? Narcissists are like predators who feed on other people's energy - they take your light, and give you their darkness. And they will show absolutely no remorse for what you are going through, but that is OK - because you will heal, and they will always be stuck in their pathological ways!

The effects of narcissistic abuse are such that avoidance feels like an escape. The constant feeling of not knowing what to expect from the narcissist is combined with low self-esteem and a feeling of utter worthlessness. Because of that, survivors feel incompetent, and view themselves the way a narcissist described them. They see themselves through narcissist's glasses and believe they will be rejected, denied and discarded, everywhere they go, and all this together causes them a lot of anxiety.

Since the abuse has damaged the core of self, survivors feel like they don't have an identity, as a relationship with a narcissist is a codependent one, and thanks to constant projection, there is no clear line to show who is who. When it all ends, many don't know who they are, feel like nothing has meaning any more, and feel powerless. Anyone who has dealt with a covert knows very well what it feels like not to be allowed to be authentic, to thrive; how it is to feel alone while being in a relationship, to feel guilty for standing up for yourself, or setting healthy boundaries. Such a person knows what it is like to be trapped in guilt for things that are not your fault, all the time; to be afraid to express yourself, and to doubt every decision you make.

Don't be ashamed if you feel this way. You are not weak; you are completely opposite. Know that you are not alone, even if it feels like it. There are others who, just like you, suffer from the effects of loving a narcissist - and they, too, feel alone. Some survivors find escape in substance abuse, some battle with sexual dysfunction, and some develop a physical illness or eating disorder due to constant stress and feeling that they're not good enough or beautiful enough. If any of this resonates with you, just don't feel "down" about yourself. Don't blame yourself because it is not your fault. These are all very human and very normal reactions to being exposed to months and years of narcissistic abuse. And most importantly, don't compare yourself to others who are able to live their life to the fullest shortly after a breakup, as the relationship you had was far from normal or healthy.

All of this happens because you suddenly start to realize whom you've dealt with, and as time goes by, things start making more sense. You start noticing your part in the game, but most importantly, you start seeing the narcissist for who he or she truly is. However, in the beginning, truth is hard to comprehend, and your mind might as well try to protect you from a flood of emotions until you're ready to face it. Unlike the narcissist, you are a healthy individual who was infected with someone else's virus, and you can get back on track and can restore your life. Even if breathing feels like a burden now, one day you will look at your relationship with them and be proud of yourself, because you will win this battle and you will endure, no matter how impossible it feels at the moment.

Chapter 12:
The road to healing

Now that you know who you have been dealing with, take a deep breather. What you've been through is something not many had to go through. A relationship with a narcissist is a trauma that leaves a mark on your body, soul, and mind, so, therefore, it may take a while to get a good grip on reality and become empowered, enlightened, and hopeful again. But I want you to know it is possible. And I want you to know it was never your fault.

You were never crazy. You were never oversensitive or naive. You dealt with a master manipulator, a mentally ill person, a devil in human form… and you feel broken for a reason.

All survivors do, and there is no shame in that. You have experienced abuse that doesn't leave marks on the body for everyone to see and understand. The sad reality survivors face during their healing journey is that no-one believes them when they say they were abused. Psychological abuse can be just as damaging as physical, but because it is invisible and leaves no bruises, survivors feel alone in their healing journey, which makes it even more painful. The abuser is not someone who had physically violent outbursts or problems with the law - they are someone who plays the role of a respectful and kind member of society.

You will slowly start to realize that you must transform from a "victim" to a "survivor" and that people you trust are just a support system, if you have any left in your life. You will come to a painful realization that this road is going to be as tough and lonesome as it usually is for survivors of narcissistic abuse. You will go through different stages of healing. After each stage you will feel better, but many times, you will swing back and forth between the stages.

There will be moments when you think you are finally getting better, only to feel paranoid or sad the next day. Don't be discouraged and hard on yourself once you do feel these waves. Healing is not a linear process, and sometimes it will feel as if you are moving one step forward and two back.

That is what all survivors go through. What you need to do in the process is to trust yourself, which can be very hard, as you are so used to doubting your thoughts, instincts and feelings. No one else was standing in your shoes and only you know what you've been through. Be prepared for people asking you why you are stuck on your "ex". Be prepared not to find understanding. Be prepared to be labeled over-dramatic, oversensitive, and be prepared to be judged - people see what the narcissist wants them to see, and it is not your job to change their mind. They will find it out themselves. So, it is time to do something you felt judged for and guilty about for so long - focus on yourself, your emotions, and your own wellbeing.

The interesting but not-so-unexpected fact I have gathered - thanks to interactions with mental health professionals - is that it is always the victim who seeks therapy, as they are aware and capable of introspection. While the narcissist, from a medical perspective, needs self-assessment and guidance from a psychologist, they rarely, if ever, get treatment for narcissism.

Their inner, malignant grandiosity is rarely, if ever spoken about, mainly because individuals with NPD, covert narcissists, believe it is the outer world to blame for all their misfortunes. They don't believe anything is wrong with them, and therefore their mental issues get projected onto their targets, who are the ones who seek help, which in itself speaks of great potential for recovery.

Chapter 13:
When does healing begin?

The healing process begins when you finally decide to cut off all contact with the narcissist, because you have seen who they truly are. You feel bad; and you want the manipulation, gaslighting and hoovering, to stop. All the signs you were ignoring and pushing under the carpet are now coming to light. Although upon cutting contact you won't necessarily label them as a narcissist, you will know enough to pull back completely. Cutting all contact with the narcissist is not like any other breakup, because a narcissist is not just any other person, and because not many "exes", friends or parents have a personality disorder. In short - healing starts when you completely abandon a narcissist. Leaving them behind and moving on happens gradually and never overnight. The first and the hardest thing to do is to accept painful reality - accepting that the narcissist never truly loved you, and was only with you because they found it convenient to feed on your energy. Once you accept the relationship was not healthy, that is where the healing process kicks in. There are three main stages you will go through: *grieving, learning,* and *rebuilding yourself.*

Grieving

Would you believe it if I told you that there is life after a narcissist? A much better life, where you wake up feeling hopeful about the future, feeling loved and appreciated? Probably not. And that is OK. After you have been abused, you can't even visualize happiness. Once it all ends, you will feel like a shadow of your former self. Like you had a chance at life and love, and you wasted it; and now you can't get back the time or find the strength to go on with your life. When they leave your life, you won't know who you are, because of all the gaslighting you have experienced. The grieving process includes a variety of emotions and is the most painful phase, being where you digest raw emotions. When grieving, you will go through the states of shock and denial, rage and anger, and depression. At this first stage, you are too drained and confused to deal with reality, and so a feeling of helplessness, deep heartache and denial, are natural responses to what you've been through. These states of mind are all entwined, come in a different order for every survivor, and you will find yourself shifting back and forth between denying what has happened and getting consumed by anger. Grieving a relationship with a healthy individual is hard. Grieving a relationship with a narcissist is ten times harder.

The first thing you will experience is denial and shock. Your body is trying to cope with the trauma that ending of a relationship with a narcissist brings. Many survivors feel the need to withdraw from the world, and can barely gather strength to leave the house. They feel immobile. Just like breaking from addiction, the first days of the withdrawal are always the worst. The pain and devastation seem unbearable. At this stage, it is important not to pressure yourself to be stronger than you are. Feel free to embrace all your negative emotions and dwell on them as much as you need. It may be tempting to go back to your old conditioning that a narcissist has thought out for you, and put yourself down, feel bad about yourself, or call yourself weak. You were taught that your emotions were not valid, that you weren't allowed to cry or feel vulnerable, for months and years, so it is healthy to put your emotions and needs first after a long, long time. Know that being able to feel is a sign of strength; and acknowledging how you feel without censoring yourself is the first step to healing.

The grieving stage is where we get angry at ourselves for allowing ourselves to be mistreated for so long, and we develop even greater anger and animosity towards our former abuser. Survivors feel deep hatred for the narcissist - to the point that it is all-consuming. And while it is a negative emotion, anger needs to be released. Being enraged and feeling hatred is a normal and healthy reaction to what we have been through. Anger is an energy, and after feeling low and completely stuck, it is when anger kicks in that survivors truly start to be more proactive on their healing journey. Many survivors I talked to explained that this anger made them change their life out of rebellion against the narcissist. You may feel like extreme injustice was done to you. You get angry at yourself for allowing them to damage you. Many survivors feel angry at not only narcissists, but all other people for causing them pain in the past, while all their suppressed anger comes to the surface. This is because your mind is slowly accepting the reality as it is, while still struggling with denial from time to time. You slowly start to see them as evil and manipulative characters, but because the truth is so painful, you will express it through anger. You may not see anger as such in the beginning, but anger is your pain and hurt transformed and expressed outward, after a very long time. It is important not to internalize the anger, or deny it. While it is overwhelming, anger is the first step in setting you free. Take the time to feel it and understand why you feel so enraged, and once you feel your anger, release it. Don't hold it in, and don't let it consume you. Holding on to anger for too long is just as toxic as staying in a relationship with a malignant individual, and gives the narcissist the power over our lives even once they are no longer part of it.

Over time, anger will dissolve, and emotions will settle. You realize how powerless you are because you can't change anything. When survivors face the painful truth of being abused, there arises an inner need to mourn. Mourn who you were. Mourn your faith in love. Mourn your capacity to trust. You feel like all faith in humanity is gone. You see all people through different lenses, and you suddenly start spotting manipulation everywhere. You were manipulated and discarded, and therefore you see the bad in people everywhere. You think everyone you deal with has ulterior motives. You see yourself as naive, and beat yourself up for allowing the narcissist to break you the way they did. You are afraid you will never be able to trust again. Ultimately, you don't feel safe. Depression is a normal part of the grieving process in every breakup, but even more so when that breakup was with a narcissist. Narcissistic abuse is toxic to one's soul and distorts the core of personality, so survivors feel as if their innocence and trust is irreversibly broken.

If you are dealing with depression during your healing process, seek help and be kind to yourself. Reach out to someone you truly trust and don't be ashamed to go to therapy if you feel the need to do so. Just like someone who's survived a car accident, you too need to mend your wounds. After being where you have, mentally and emotionally, you will need to allow yourself to lean on someone; because you were demanded to be strong for so long, for someone who never appreciated it and never will. Try to surround yourself with everything that matters to you, even if it's only your pet. You have gone so far and endured so much. It is OK to feel the way you feel, and it is OK to feel helpless.

An inability to move, hatred, anger and depressive episodes, will all be prominent until the end of the grieving stage. You will likely shift from feeling rebellious and suddenly empowered, to feeling devastated, very quickly. This is emotional cleansing, the process where your emotional body tries to re-balance itself by adapting to a new reality. By feeling all those emotions, you are actually cleansing your mind from the toxicity you lived in. Everything you feel on an internal level at this point is a result of subconscious realization - the realization that who you loved, or still think you do, is not who or what you thought them to be.

As paradoxical as it seems, normal life without a narcissist may feel abnormal at times, especially if you dealt with them for years! Your emotional self was conditioned to react based on certain patterns that are unnatural to mentally healthy individuals, so once the covert is gone, your whole system needs to rewire, and this will happen slowly as time goes by. It will happen by gradually going through all the emotions, and feeling what you need to feel. There will be days you miss them, and days when you can't stop thinking about how much you love them. As a relationship with someone who has an NPD is a constant rollercoaster, and the whole relationship is built on false ideals and illusions, it is natural to ponder over the relationship. It is not easy to erase all the positive memories you had with the narcissist, as these will pop into your consciousness every now and then. You may hold onto the good times you had with them, cherish good memories, and find yourself missing them deeply.

If that is so, be kind to yourself. You, unlike the narcissist, are capable of love. If you find yourself looking back on happy times with them, know that such thoughts are normal, as getting over someone you cared truly about, even when you know they are bad for you, is not an easy thing to do. Feel everything you need to feel. Don't react, don't call them, just feel. Take the time you need to mourn the loss of someone you loved, and even more, to mourn the illusions that kept you imprisoned for so long. Don't push yourself into anything. The next stage, where you start gaining more clarity and better grasp of your emotions, will come naturally once you are ready, whenever that may be for you.

Learning

At this stage, answers slowly start coming to consciousness - what you have been dealing with is a narcissist. Claire, who was married to a narcissist for seventeen years, emailed me this:

When I first found the term "narcissist", my first reaction was a negation. He wasn't the type to ever call himself successful or handsome. He was never boastful about his achievements. But what I found strange is that some of the traits did fit him. I always felt like he lacked empathy, and he did make me feel guilty and bad about myself. I really did feel like I was nothing next to him. I just didn't click well with the stereotypical description of a narcissist, at first. It wasn't until I came across the term "covert narcissism" when I truly found the answer I needed. I remember I kept reading article after article, forum after forum, with my eyes wide open. I was shocked. This is what I was dealing with. Stories of other survivors resembled mine so much, to the point I remember whispering to myself - yes, yes, this is it! Suddenly I didn't feel alone. There are some other people who dealt with the same stuff as I did. Everything made so much sense.

Many survivors first start off thinking the relationship is just toxic. If you dealt with a narcissist, you probably knew all along there was something "off" in the relationship, but couldn't pinpoint exactly what that was. There is an unexplainable feeling that something isn't right, and it is this feeling that awakens the investigative spirit in survivors. Answers are soothing, especially because a relationship with a narcissist is such that there are not many needful things said, understood, spoken about, and discussed. When you finally don't have someone over your shoulder to call you oversensitive, dramatic or crazy for demanding answers, you can finally start searching for them on your own. More often than not, those who were victims of a covert narcissist do find out about the term "narcissism". It is when we truly reflect on the relationship, without being gaslighted and clouded by emotions any more, that the learning phase starts.

The phase of learning is closely entwined with grieving the relationship. It is in this stage that survivors truly start seeking answers, both from within, and from the exterior world, by learning, studying psychology or spirituality. This is not to say that grieving wasn't part of the learning process. On the contrary. The grieving process is learning on a subconscious level, cleansing, and preparation for learning about who it is that you dealt with, in order to understand why you feel the way you do. The second stage is when learning becomes more focused and more of a conscious process. Powered by anger, remorse, and depression, you may be overwhelmed by the need to understand why. While the previous stage was colored by remembrance of the narcissist, the learning stage is when rumination and analyzing intensifies. You feel the need to understand every motive behind their behaviors, but now, because there is no more gaslighting to cloud your judgment, you can see the relationship and the narcissist more clearly. Finding answers may seem like a chain of "epiphanies", sudden realizations that are both shocking and eye-opening.

Trying to find the answers is always combined with feelings returning sporadically and in different intensities, which is why this is the stage of both clarity and confusion. Many survivors reported they had sleepless nights of "overthinking" and found it very hard to focus on anything other than what they experienced. Understanding why the covert narcissist behaved the way they did becomes a focus, a healthy focus that will bring more light to previously clouded judgment. This need to understand steams from the very gaslighting and manipulation survivors have been exposed to. Because all their emotions have come to the surface, and survivors have not experienced any further shaming, blaming, or more gaslighting, there is more space for analysis in order to decode narcissistic behavior. With time, you will see narcissistic patterns of behavior more clearly and will be able to distinguish between who you are, and who they are. You were in love with an illusion! When you are ready, you will finally accept the truth as it is.

Increased consciousness can result in labeling everyone around us as toxic, narcissistic, manipulative and controlling. This is a natural generalization that we form as a result of learning. Through educating ourselves, we digest new knowledge, and find it easier to spot it in people's behavior. While a result of increased knowledge can be like paranoia, stemming from past traumatic experiences with the narcissist, such generalization is a preparation for truly seeing and rapidly recognizing manipulative behavior in the future. Suddenly, you will start to see things clearly. Those "Aha!" moments will shake you out of the numbness of the previous stage.

By the end of this phase, you will no longer feel trapped in a whirlpool of cognitive dissonance (i.e. feeling one thing and knowing another at the same time) and you will be able to discern what your own thought patterns are, and what are just those that were projected onto you. There will be less duality and more clarity in your life: you will trust yourself more. Reflecting on happy moments with the narcissist will occur. As mental fog disappears, you will be able to slowly gain more control over your life, and the image of perfect love you thought you had, will slowly start to fade. As you learn more about how to deal with the pain, how to heal from depression, or how to control anger, you will start empowering yourself, discovering who the narcissist is at their core, and most importantly, who you are. As you gain clarity, either through introspection and self-searching, or through therapy, you will reconnect with yourself and form a foundation to rebuild yourself once again, forming much stronger personal boundaries than you ever had. If, during the learning stage, you feel guarded and closed off to other people, know that this is a natural and necessary defensive response. Follow your natural compass and listen to what your inner self is trying to guide you to do.

You will regain strength through embracing negative emotions, through self-observation, support, and self-care, experiencing the first waves of stabilization, safety, and enlightenment within. Self-education, self-help and therapy, will give you great insights into false beliefs you had, what your defense mechanisms are, and you will defeat fears that the narcissist has projected onto you. After being mentally, physically, spiritually and emotionally abused, you will slowly come to realize you have faced and survived one of the greatest, most damaging energies there are. Narcissistic abuse is one of the most traumatic experiences, but it is also where you learn how powerful you are. After suffering for so long, being afraid, feeling mad or unworthy, you will come to see that you have actually faced the worst life has to offer - and this will make you fierce and fearless. It takes a lot of personal power and a strong character to defeat the darkness imposed by a narcissist, and the very fact that you are here, reading this content, speaks of how determined to rise and heal you are. And trust me when I say, you will.

Rebuilding yourself

The grieving phase ends with acceptance. Eventually, you get tired of feeling the way you do. Great injustice had been done to you, and it is normal to be angry at yourself and life. Once you accept that you were dealing with an unhealthy individual, who isn't what you thought they are, things truly begin to shift. It is hard to accept that love you thought was strong, was all just an illusion. It is hard to accept, for example with a parent, that someone who raised you is someone who never truly wished you well. These are hard truths and they are hard to digest. But once you realize what really happened behind the curtains, you'll be relieved that it was never about you. It is a bumpy road and it takes a lot of courage and patience with yourself to get to the point when you can fully acknowledge what has transpired. You come to terms with your past and accept that no amount of anger, remorse or hatred, will change it.

Acceptance feels like a huge burden was lifted from your shoulders. It is when you finally take personal responsibility for the part you played - without judging yourself for allowing yourself to take part in it. Know that every reaction back then was the best reaction you could have made. You did the best you could in given circumstances. You didn't know you were loving a covert narcissist until they broke you, and you didn't have the experience you have now, back then, to do any differently. And while the first two stages are crawling down the road to moving on, it is in this third stage when you start feeling like yourself again, and can finally gallop forward, feeling as if you have truly moved on. Moving on is empowering because it minimizes the narcissist and their importance.

As unrealistic as it seems, especially if you are at the beginning phases of healing from narcissistic abuse, there will be a moment in your healing journey when the focus shifts from the narcissist and the pain - to you. They took so much mental and emotional space in your being, that now they are gone, you can finally fill it with something that helps you feel good about yourself, grow, and expand as a person. A narcissist has an impact on us long after the relationship ends. Once we choose to forgive ourselves and forgive our abusers, it is when we truly find peace within, and take away the power a narcissist had over us and over our lives. A narcissist is not someone who can ever change, who can ever grow, love or trust themselves. Many survivors find it difficult to forgive, and that is OK. Something as torturous as emotional or physical abuse is not an easy thing to forgive. However, in the end, the only thing that needs to remain with us are the lessons we learned.

Once this experience is behind you, and you no longer feel the heaviness in your heart, you will suddenly feel light. You will feel peaceful. You will have all the answers you need. You don't see yourself as a victim, but rather a survivor. You pity the narcissist, and it will be because you pity them for being unable to ever have a meaningful relationship. This is when you let go. Letting go and moving on means finally defeating the abuser and defeating the darkness that was imposed on you. By moving on, you devalue and defeat the narcissist, minimize their importance, and gain control over your own life again. Pain, doubt, and remorse no longer have power over you, and neither does the abuser you once dealt with.

Maybe you won't look at people the same way. Maybe you will become much more cautious and much more realistic, but maybe that is all good for you. Dealing with a narcissist is one of the toughest life lessons one can be put through, but it is also a lesson that builds you up to be more resilient to any form of manipulation in the future. It makes you tougher and more aware of what people are capable of. However, it is by finding the courage to love and trust again that we finally defeat the one who made us believe all people are vile, cruel and manipulative. What you need to know is that you are not the same person you were, and that this is a good thing. Don't be fearful of new connections. Once you pass the first two stages of your healing journey and get to the third, you will see things from a much different perspective. Use your knowledge about narcissism to build yourself and strengthen yourself. By this stage, when a manipulator or a narcissist crosses your path, you will know. But what you will also learn, by putting yourself first and blocking off toxic people from your life, is that there are people who just like you, are capable of building loving, meaningful relationships.

By being courageous and loving anew, you prove the narcissist has not damaged you. Your ability to care and love for people is what makes the difference between you and them. It is by trusting anew, rather than building walls around your heart, that you will finally be able to make new, healthy relationships. Relationships you deserve, with people who deserve you. Once you take back personal power, and rebuild yourself through learning from such adversity and hardship the narcissist has put you through, you will become stronger than you ever were before. Being treated the way you were is a painful lesson that teaches you how to stand up for yourself, how to love yourself, and how you should never compromise your feelings so as to try to make someone else love you or feel better. Narcissistic abuse teaches us authenticity, and how important we and our needs are, in the most brutal, torturous way; so if you have survived it, you should be proud of yourself. You have been through hell and you made your way through it. It is proof of your personal strength and character. A relationship with a narcissist is a power play, and when we choose to heal, it is when we finally win.

Chapter 14:
How to deal with a narcissist

There are no greater teachers than personal experience, knowledge, and awareness. Cutting off all contact with the narcissist is the best possible scenario that speeds up the healing process. However, much of the time relationships with them are not so simple, and there are other people or factors involved, such as children, colleagues, shared property, workplace or family members. More so, because narcissists can be parents of our children, our siblings or bosses, so instead we will have to plan on minimizing contact with them because we are forced to have encounters with them, sometimes daily.

The following are the last pages of the book. I hope its content has given you fruitful thoughts and made you feel less alone in your healing journey. In the very end, I have prepared a few useful tips that can ease your life, and prevent more hardship and pain that you might get from a narcissist at this time. In case you are still dealing with one in your private life or in the workplace, and are looking for the best way to manage your relationship, especially when cutting off all contact is out of the equation, here is what you can do to keep yourself as sane as possible.

Awareness

When you are aware of their narcissistic behavior and have figured out their patterns, what you can do is use this awareness to your advantage. Once you can see through the narcissist, and accept who he or she is, you can predict their reactions and therefore use the knowledge to manipulate the situation in your favor. This does not mean becoming a narcissist yourself. What it simply means is protecting yourself from the abuser by knowing how they abuse. You know the narcissist is there for narcissistic supply, and you know that these people never change. What can change is your approach. Study your narcissist, observe them, and spot the behavioral scheme they have. Knowing how they work, and understanding that they are self-serving people with what psychologists term "cluster B disorder", incapable of empathy, won't directly change how they treat you very much. But what will change is how you perceive them and react to them. This will minimize the mental and emotional damage they can do to you. Nothing they do is ever about you, or anyone else, it is always about them. Knowing and understanding this, and accepting that you cannot change or enlighten them, will save you from future injury, and giving in to any temptation to play their games.

Passivity and disengagement

Covert narcissists are never mindful of your needs, so trying to explain your point of view, communicate your feelings or seek understanding from them is only going to give them more material to manipulate you. Don't try to seek justice or communicate with them as with others, because there is no space for compromise, tolerance, or a peaceful resolution - unless it suits them at the moment. The best way to actively handle blame-games and gaslighting is first, to be aware of them; and second, to play along. For instance, when they blame you for being selfish, just tell them: *You are right, I am so selfish.* I agree with everything the narcissist says. If they are trying to convince you that you've done something you know you haven't, then you can play along with, *Oh yes, you are right. I remember I did that.* In this way you turn their weapon, gaslighting and manipulation, against them, because they are perfectly aware (just like you are) that you never did what they accused you of. A narcissist is not a healthy individual, and this admittedly unauthentic act can protect you from being controlled by them. In the process, always be mindful of your actions and know who you are dealing with, in order to protect your personal integrity.

Another thing you can do when you notice their behavior making you feel heavyhearted or hurt, is to simply disengage and detach yourself from the situation by being aware of who you are really dealing with. Part of the disengagement technique includes self-discipline. When something feels wrong, don't try to find out why: just distance yourself from the situation. A narcissist communicates from an ego-centered place, and asking for explanations will only bring you more confusion and headache. Trust yourself enough, that the very feeling that something is not right is enough for you to leave the situation. Do so by acting out peacefully and kindly, without explaining yourself, so as not to give the narcissist space to pull you back into the drama.

Privacy protection
Dealing with a sick individual demands a lot of mindfulness and awareness. What gives narcissists the power to control their targets is knowing their character, being able to predict their behaviors, and being aware of what makes them tick. That is why protecting yourself from narcissistic abuse in the future means keeping your life as private as possible. Don't let them know how you feel, what you fear, or what you hope for. Distance yourself as much as you can, and don't get them involved in your life. This will create a necessary barrier as

they won't be able to manipulate your feelings when they don't know what matters to you. Keep the narcissist informed only on very basic things, such as moving locations when still sharing custody over children, or keeping it strictly professional in the workplace.

Self-empowerment

In the end, there is nothing that defeats the narcissist more and protects you from them, than having firm personal boundaries. This is something you will find easier to do by the end of the third stage of healing, so be patient with yourself. These skills are built slowly and require some practice. While not an easy road, once we are aware of it, narcissistic abuse teaches us to protect ourselves and prioritize our needs. Developing skills to cope with narcissism in others also includes practicing self-awareness, includes knowing and accepting your own vulnerability without feeling flawed or weak. Being vulnerable means being human. This allows you to accept yourself and leaves no space for someone to devalue you. Don't be afraid to say "no" when things don't feel right. There is no need to explain yourself, especially when dealing with a covert narcissist. Assert your boundaries calmly and don't ever feel bad for doing so. Saying "no" isn't selfish; actually it's healthy. The narcissist will probably try to pull you into their drama, so be aware of guilt-tripping and stay strong in your integrity. You are *not responsible* for someone else's happiness. You are *not expected* to give your time and resources selflessly. Trust yourself enough to walk away from things that don't feel good. It is OK and healthy to put yourself first. It is OK not to respond when you don't feel like it. Love is never restricting or conditional. Love is not abuse. Love feels good.

Being open to love, being giving and helpful, are great virtues and should be cherished. These are virtues that will help you create balanced, healthy relationships in the future, with a healthy individual who is able to reciprocate your love equally. Narcissists don't know how to appreciate it, and they give themselves permission to take it for granted and misuse it; and that is not your fault. Not everyone is worthy of your love, and no-one should ever cost you your peace of mind.

You are lovable. You are strong, otherwise, you wouldn't be here. And you are much more than you were told you are. One day, you will make it through. Life will be much more different, and a narcissist won't cause you pain any more. Once you get there, just remember to give yourself credit for it. Through adversity, we grow.

Conclusion

Everyone who ever dealt with a covert narcissist knows the pain, toxicity, and the hardships such an individual brings. As a result of being exposed to narcissistic abuse for a prolonged period of time, victims, future survivors, face many challenges and are faced with a great task. They have to leave it all behind, and try to heal from what has occurred as a result of that relationship. Healing from abuse is never easy because cruelty leaves deep, humiliating marks on one's personality and diminishes one's wellbeing. Covert narcissism is a set of destructive behavioral patterns that harm everyone involved with a person who harbors these attitudes. Unfortunately, because it is a personality disorder that has to be understood and its presence sensed, there are no proven ways to foresee you are dealing with one, unless you've experienced being abused by a narcissist in your past.

Being so hard to diagnose, covert narcissists, because they are usually so well-liked and accepted in society, represent a real threat to everyone they are involved with, as their destructive patterns, manipulation techniques and controlling behavior can be extremely damaging to one's mental, physical, and emotional health. Being part of the infamous Cluster B spectrum of personality disorders, covert narcissism represents a real danger to one's sense of self, one's self-worth and mental health in general. It is threatening and it is disturbing, which is why a healing process for those who suffered from narcissistic abuse will be a lengthy process that is never light and easy.

Covert narcissists violate, deceive, abuse and exploit those they form bonds with, and they do so meticulously hidden behind the mask of loving, empathetic individuals who serve society. Their sense of extreme grandiosity and lack of empathy make a combination that allows them to heartlessly hurt, lie and discard those who are unfortunate enough to love them - and they do so without guilt or remorse. Projection, gaslighting, blaming and withdrawing affection, all leave their victims feeling drained, empty and lifeless, where they can barely gather strength for performing basic daily activities. Because it is not so frequently spoken about, diagnosed or treated, and because it is so cunningly concealed, survivors of narcissistic abuse are frequently left to deal with the effects of a relationship with such malicious, toxic individuals on their own. It is encouraging to hear that there is a rising number of past victims, now survivors, who are willing to bring more light onto the subject of narcissism, share their experiences and testimonies, which proves that there are more victims out there than was believed. It is in awareness and acceptance, acting individually and globally, where a real battle against both abuse and abuser begins, so narcissism - above all covert narcissism - should never be spoken about lightly.

This personality disorder is gravely harmful to others, but with healing, therapy and learning about it, its effects can decrease over time, paving a path to a brighter, better future, away from the narcissist. This book I wrote is one of the tools that is meant to help those who had, or still have, a covert narcissist in their lives, and along with other techniques and resources, it will hopefully shine more light on narcissistic personality disorder, what its effects are, and what brings healing from it. Together, we can make covert narcissism more visible, and we can win against it. No one who is trying to heal is alone on their journey, as there are many others who feel the same and have been down a similar road. The path of healing is not easy, but it is possible and it is worthwhile. Most importantly - you can and will heal. Your covert may have won a few battles, but they will never win the war because they don't have the emotional and mental capacity to do so. But you do.

In unity and with knowledge, we can defeat the invisible enemy and rise above it all.

Author's Note

Dear reader,

I hope you enjoyed my book.

Please don't forget to toss up a quick review on amazon, I will personally read it! Positive or negative, I'm grateful for all feedback.

Reviews are so helpful for self-published authors and your feedback can make such a difference for my book!

Thanks very much for your time, and I look forward to hearing from you soon.

Sincerely,

Theresa

Printed in Great Britain
by Amazon